How to
Self-Publish
a
Children's Paperback
Picture Book
using
Amazon
Kindle Direct Publishing (KDP)
- an Overview -

Other titles by this author:
We Eat Food That's Fresh, with Companion CD
Comemos Comida Fresca, English & Spanish
We Love the Company, A Book About Table Manners, with Companion CD
When You Find Colors and Shapes
Cuando Encuentres los Colores y las Formas, English & Spanish
Fruits & Veggies Row by Row, English
Fruits & Veggies Making Faces, English

About the Author:
Angela Russ-Ayon resides in Long Beach, California, with her family.
She is a keynote speaker and trainer on the subject of early childhood development,
and owner of the Russ InVision Company record label, which boasts over
1.5 million in sales, has been presented 9 early childhood music awards
of excellence, and whose music is represented by school suppliers nationwide.
Her specialty is engaging young children in interactive song and dance using fine and gross motor
activities that promote imaginative play, bridge educational gaps, and help build brain pathways.

Primary Illustrator: José Gascón H.

Edited by Anna Cayot

ISBN-13: 978-0-9987090-4-8

1st edition

For information about permission to reproduce selections of this book, contact:

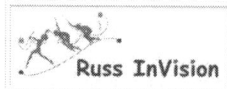

Russ InVision

Russ InVision Company
3219 Conquista Ave., Long Beach, CA 90808
E-mail: info@abridgeclub.com
www.abridgeclub.com
Author: Angela Russ-Ayon

Library of Congress Control Number: 2019901904

Author's NOTE

Thank you for your time and interest in my book. It is designed to be a basic overview of self-publishing a picture book that you can hold in your hands and includes aspects that I feel are important to share, especially with young writers. Did I leave some things out? Absolutely. I touched on aspects of publishing that would typically take many more pages to explain, and I was not able to provide examples for everything. If you have a question about a topic, I encourage you to broaden your knowledge base with supplemental research. There are some excellent articles and books that delve deeper into writing, illustrating, and publishing to help you improve your skills.

Expect links and tips to change as Amazon KDP continues to update their webpage. I will certainly try to keep up.

I welcome your constructive criticism, comments, observations, and questions.

I can't wait to read your book!

- Angela
www.AbridgeClub.com

TABLE of CONTENTS

The PICTURE BOOK

Picture books come in all shapes and sizes and can be for any age. They are specially designed to help children develop their reading skills. So they have basic vocabulary young children can understand but not necessarily read. Picture books can easily be identified by their characteristics:

- pictures (illustration) with storytelling qualities
- pictures represent, but do not mirror the text
- limited number of words
- lyrical language with pleasing rhythm
- larger than average print
- usually 32 pages
- a size that will fit on a standard bookshelf, though some are published as BIG books.

Some picture books are **textless** and have no words at all. Children gather information from the pictures and interpret the story solely by inferring and using reasoning skills. As they notice more details, their interpretation of the story changes. The great thing about textless books is that they can be enjoyed whether people can read or not.

The Picture Book AUDIENCE

Most picture books are published for an audience of young readers who are in preschool through first grade, but all ages enjoy them.

Children from newborns to five-year-olds depend on pictures in books to understand a story. In these cases, adults do all of the reading and explain any difficult words or concepts.

First, second, and third graders who can read for themselves still read picture books, but their books typically have more words in them and the illustration is downsized to make room for more text. Their books can have as many as 45 pages or more.

The term "children" is very broad. Decide who your audience will be because you can't write for everyone. Choose a specific age group and get to know those children very well.

- Read bestsellers they read. Discover what interests and entertains them.
- Read online reviews for popular children's books.
- Volunteer to read in class and at libraries to see how children respond to different books.
- Study the elements of each story by writing them on story maps.

SELF-PUBLISHING

When **self-publishing** a book, you do all of the work yourself, without any help from an established, professional traditional publishing house. You handle the entire book publication process with total control and creative freedom. Even though there are certain standards in the industry, no one can tell you what you can and can't do. You set the price of your own book, keeping it reasonable and competitive with other books on the market. You don't have to sign any exclusive contracts, and you can publish very fast, receiving a physical copy of your book as soon as seven to ten days after it goes live on Amazon.com. You can even discount books to negotiate special deals with customers.

Self-publishing a picture book includes:

- Writing your story
- Editing your story
- Illustrating your story
- Laying the text around your illustration
- Formatting your book for printing
- Paying for printing
- Selling your book
- Distributing your book to stores that want to resell it
- Marketing and promoting yourself and your book.

There are many different **self-publishing companies** available to authors who want to publish their own books. Some specialize in a few specific services and others give you an entire package. Some resources you pay for, and others are free if you know where to look. **Amazon KDP is a full-service self-publishing platform that publishes for free**. It offers free online tutorials to help you get your book published on their website. KDP also offers special services for a fee, but you don't have to use them unless you can't figure out how to do something yourself.

AMAZON Kindle Direct Publishing (KDP)

Amazon KDP specializes in **print-on-demand (POD)** and commonly works with authors who want to print any quantity of books. POD is a way of digitally printing books only as you need them, or after readers purchase. KDP does not turn authors away because they don't like their stories. They will print almost any book you submit as long as you have followed their guidelines:

- format the book correctly
- upload the files properly
- publish original work

Otherwise, there is little, if any, out of pocket cost or financial risk to publishing with KDP. You get paid after you sell something, and KDP takes a percentage of every book sold based on how much the book costs to print.

Retail stores all over the world can purchase books from Amazon KDP at a discounted price for resale in their online store, or one with a physical address. Stores with a physical address, like Barnes and Noble, are called "brick and mortar" stores, but like Barnes and Noble, many retailers also sell online.

Here are a few benefits of self-publishing using Amazon KDP.

- Publish books to Amazon within 7-days or less and see how they sell over time.
- Order any number of books when you want them.
- Revise the story, cover, or price.
- No need to order large quantities, like 2,400 books, that sit around for years and years.
- Purchase books for resale from KDP at a discounted author's price that you can use for giveaways, promotions, signings, book fairs, and other sales.
- Amazon deals with the customers and process all orders.
- Exposure to readers and retailers all around the world.

Authors are able to order just enough books to sign at a book fair or share with friends and family. If someone wants to buy books, an author can place an order to have any number of books shipped directly from KDP to the customer at a discounted author's cost.

For example, authors can buy books from Amazon KDP at a discounted author's cost of say... $3.70, then re-sell their books at a book fair or book signing for whatever price they want.

KDP ROYALTIES

A **royalty** is a percentage of money paid to the author and illustrator for books sold. After self-published books are sold and shipped through Amazon KDP, Amazon pays the authors. It is that simple. There are two ways to get paid for self-publishing books.

1. Amazon KDP sells books online and pays authors approximately 60 days after the end of the month in which the books were sold. For example, KDP pays authors a percentage of the purchase price at the end of March for books sold in January. This is not negotiable. It does no good to call or email Amazon KDP and ask for your money after your books are sold, no matter how many were purchased.

Amazon KDP sends checks to authors when they owe the authors $100 or more, or they will directly deposit money of any amount into an author's bank account.

2. The author orders books online at KDP and pays the discounted author price to KDP. The author directs KDP on where to ship the books, either directly to their customer or directly to the author. The author collects a payment from the customer.

Authors set the retail price for their books with KDP. The **retail price** is the total price charged for the book sold to a customer, which includes the cost to make the book and the money earned from the sale. There are a few limitations, but the pricing is pretty straight forward. When you set up your book on the KDP online system and enter a retail price, KDP calculates what your royalty will be. Here are examples of two different pricing structures for a 32-page color picture book. One is for a book selling for $12.99, and the other is for a book selling for $10.99; however, KDP royalties are subject to change.

- KDP sells book for $12.99

- KDP pays author $4.14 royalty

= Author can buy book for $3.65 + Shipping

- KDP sells book for $10.00

- KDP pays author $2.35 royalty

- Author can buy book for $3.65 + Shipping

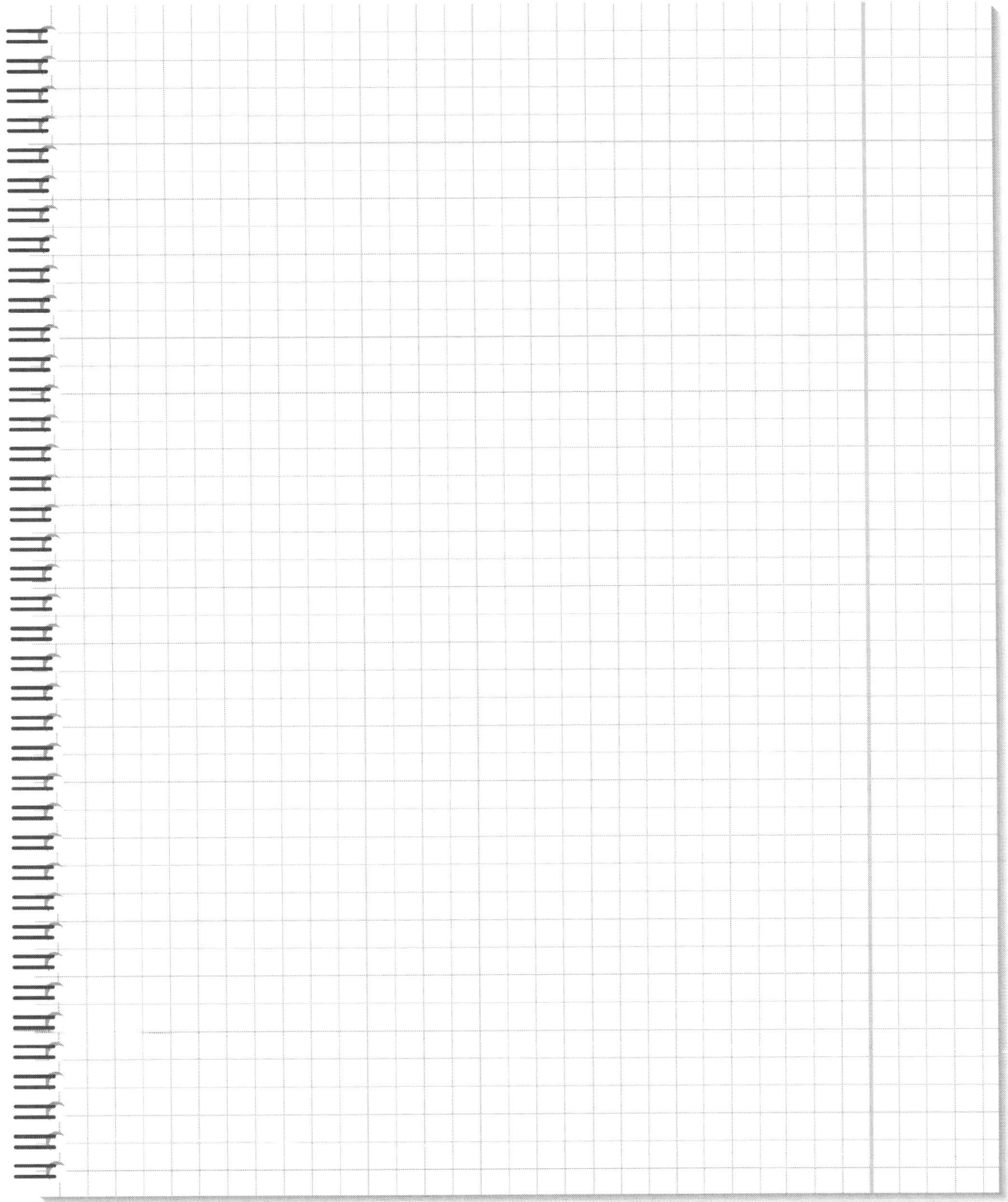

TRADITIONAL PUBLISHING HOUSES

Self-publishing has become very popular, but we can't talk about self-publishing without talking about publishing the traditional way. A **traditional publishing house** is a professional company that specializes in publishing books. An editor at the publishing house reviews the book and decides whether to offer the writer a deal for the rights to print the book.

Amazon KDP is not a traditional publisher. If you are self-publishing, you don't have to worry about this side of the publishing industry, but it is worth informing you about, just the same.

Once a book is finished, an author chooses whether to either self-publish the book or submit the manuscript to a traditional publishing house. A **manuscript** is an original book, document, or piece of music written by hand or typed, that has not been published. If you have finished your book, you have a manuscript. Most manuscripts don't include illustrations. Traditional publishing houses typically assign illustrators to complete the artwork for books.

The review process at a traditional publishing house can take anywhere from three to 12 months, depending on the size of the company. Publishing houses receive hundreds of books each month. When they offer an author a deal, the deal is based on how well the editor thinks the author's book will sell. In exchange for the rights to publish and sell the book, the publishing house pays the author an advance on future royalties.

Traditional publishing houses specialize in particular categories. Their specialties encompass recipe books, magazines, children's books, novels, comic books, and more. Within each category, a publisher might also specialize in a genre. A **genre** is a particular category of book, like science fiction, thriller, horror, comedy, action and adventure, romance, autobiography, and so on. Within their genres, they get even more specific, and might only sell young adult science fiction, or baby board books.

Every publisher has specific guidelines to follow and a website where you can gather more information. Another resource worth adding to your library is a book called *The Writer's Market,* which is updated and published every year to help authors and illustrators navigate around the publishing industry. Among other things, it includes contacts, submission information, and listings for book publishers, consumer magazines, trade magazines, contests, and awards.

What does a traditional publishing house do? Depending upon the size, it does a lot.

- Checks the book for errors and story issues.
- Hires an illustrator to design a winning cover and interior artwork.
- Formats the book so that it prints correctly.
- Pays for printing the book and all other publishing expenses.
- Promotes and publicizes the author and the book.
- Keeps track of sales and accounting.
- Makes sure the book gets into retail "brick and mortar" or online stores.
- Continues to print and distribute the books to stores.

An author who sells thousands of self-published books has leverage when and if he or she decides to approach a literary agent or a traditional publisher about a contract. If the author gets very popular by self-publishing, a representative from a traditional publishing house may come knocking and make a really nice offer to publish the book. These days, so many authors are publishing on their own, that big publishers play a waiting game to see which self-published authors come out on top of the heap.

Even a traditional publishing house expects its authors to promote and publicize their books by building a website, writing blogs, visit schools, boosting their social media presence, and so forth. Nowhere on Earth can authors just sit back and wait for their book to become a best seller.

The ADVANCE

How does an established traditional publishing house pay authors and illustrators?

An **advance** is the money paid to the author and illustrator by a traditional publishing house at the beginning of the publishing process, sometimes in installments. Think of it as the money (royalty) paid "in advance" or before a book goes to print. Most publishers calculate the advance based on how many books they think they will sell in the first six to twelve months after a book is on the market. Average advances run between $1000 and $15,000 per book, but bestselling authors typically get paid more.

Authors who are new to the market do not usually get a huge advance. When J. K. Rowling first published *Harry Potter and the Philosopher's Stone*, she made a deal with a small traditional publisher named Bloomsbury to print 500 copies for a £2,500 advance, which is approximately $3,198 in United States dollars. No one would offer her that amount now.

On occasion, authors and illustrators are paid a flat fee for their work, which means they are paid one specified amount and that's all. Though this is rare, it does happen when authors and illustrators are hired to write something specific. The only issue is that neither one gets to benefit from the success of the book if it is indeed successful.

Amazon KDP does not pay advances to authors or illustrators.

Well-known athletes, models, actors, actresses, talk show hosts, politicians, social media influencers, and other famous people receive high advances for their books because they are popular enough to attract lots of attention.

It is easier for famous people to promote their books since they already have a large following of fans. . Fans want to meet them, so they come to their signings and buy books for autographs. They are also welcome on talk shows and radio shows because of who they are and what they do.

The ROYALTIES

As books sell, traditional publishing houses pay a **royalty**, or a percentage of money, to the author and illustrator. If a book sells for $10.00 in the store, and the traditional publisher pays a 10% royalty to the author, then the author earns 10% of $10.00, or $1.00 for every book sold in the store. If an author has been paid a $1000 advance, then the author will first need to earn $1,000 in royalties from sales of the book to cover the advance before receiving any additional royalties. As long as the book is still in print and selling, the author continues to receive royalty checks on a regular basis. Why is the royalty such a small percentage? The publisher is taking all of the risks and responsibilities of costs, time, and manpower to design, print, distribute, transport, and market the book.

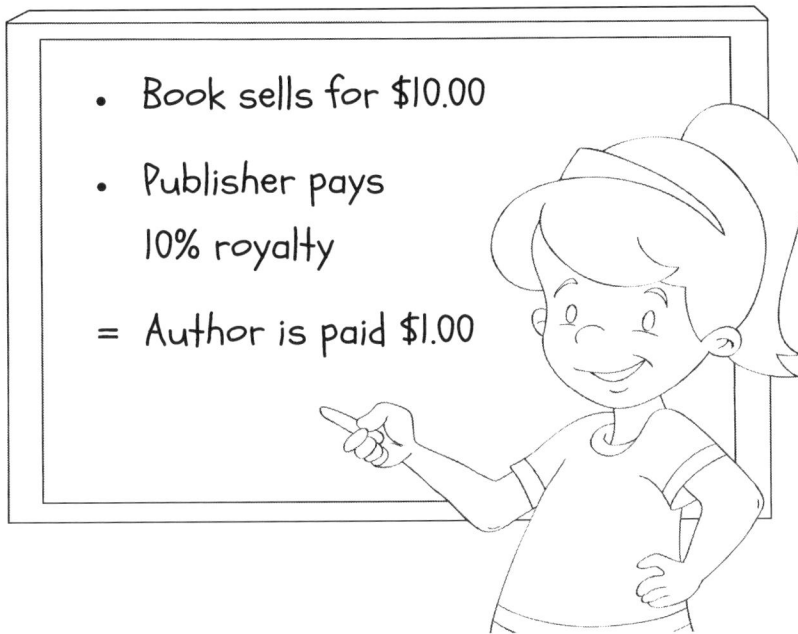

- Book sells for $10.00
- Publisher pays 10% royalty
= Author is paid $1.00

Authors and illustrators may also be represented by **literary agents** who have a relationship with traditional publishing houses. These agents are "in the know" and can get books reviewed faster than if an author sends the book directly to the publishing house without representation. If the agent is any good, the publisher respects his or her opinion about the book. Using an agent is like the difference between showing up at a party with an invitation, and showing up at a party hoping someone will recognize you and let you in the door. If the author has an agent, the author pays the agent 10% to 15% commission on every book sold.

FICTION or NONFICTION?

What are you going to write about? Think like your audience. No matter who you're writing for, your story should have a beginning, a middle, and a satisfying ending.

FICTION

If your story is **fiction**, then it was created from your imagination. It doesn't matter what the subject of your book is. If you made it up, then it is fiction. A fiction story has the following elements:

- **Plot**: the main events of the story.
- **Characters**: the people, animals, or imaginary in the story.
- **Setting**: The time when and place where the story happens.
- **Theme**: The main message of the story.

The first thing you need when you write a picture book is a good **idea**. You will probably come up with many ideas that you won't use, but don't give up. Think! An adult caregiver, like a parent or teacher, will be buying the book. Will an adult want to read what you wrote to a child? Will a child want to listen to what you wrote? Is there a life-lesson in the story? Are you teaching a child something that's important to know?

Common THEMES

Pick a theme to which many readers can relate. A **theme** is the main idea or topic of your story. The theme doesn't have to be original. The same issues and life-lessons pop up in children's books all of the time. Your success will depend upon how unique and captivating your approach is. You can also come up with a new topic. Tell your story not just to one child, but to the masses.

Here are some common themes for children's picture books:

- A parent's love is endless
- There are different types of families
- Community helpers are our friends
- An act of kindness can change a life
- Material possessions are not as important as friendship
- Differences can bring us together
- Rumors and gossip can hurt people
- We are all the same on the inside
- Work hard for what you want
- Healthy and exercise are important
- It's what's inside a person that matters

- Honesty is the best policy
- Practice makes you better
- Education is important
- Working hard pays off
- Don't judge a book by it's cover
- Accepting who you are
- Everyone needs a friend
- Sharing is caring
- Anti-bullying
- Good sportsmanship
- Belonging
- Never give up
- Patience is a virtue
- Words can hurt
- Care for the planet
- Fear of the dark
- Good hygiene
- Moving away
- Specific illnesses
- Dealing with loss and grief

The GENRE

As mentioned before, a **genre** is a particular category of a book such as mystery, science fiction, fantasy, comedy, love and friendship, thriller, and horror. Choose a genre and be true to it. Fans of certain genres expect to read about certain things. Readers who like horror hope to get scared. Readers who prefer mysteries expect a riddle to figure out or a secret to uncover. Readers who like adventure want an exciting, and possibly perilous, experience.

SCIENCE
DISCOVERY

ACTION
ADVENTURE
THRILLER

SCIENCE FICTION
TIME TRAVEL
SPACE EXPLORATION
ALIENS

MYSTERY
CRIME-SOLVING

MAGIC & WIZARDRY
MYTHICAL CREATURES
FANTASY

NATURE
ANIMALS
INSECTS

AREAS of
PERSONAL
INTEREST
and
EXPERIENCES

The PLOT

A story doesn't exist without a plot of some kind and there is no rule that says you have to follow a traditional plot. The **plot** is the storyline of the text, or the main events of the story written in sequence. As a matter of fact, some authors have broken the rules and found success in doing it. Whatever your plot, it should be easy to follow. Find a way to interest the readers and keep them turning pages, guessing what the next move will be.

Here is an example of a **traditional plot**:

- Introduce the main character
- Introduce the setting of the story.
- Bring in the conflict or problem.
- The conflict escalates or the problem gets worse.
- The main character tries to resolve the conflict.
- The conflict is as bad as it can get.
- The main character resolves the conflict.

The CHARACTERS

There should be a memorable and well-developed **main character** that is the major focus of the story. It can be a person, an animal, an insect, an alien, or an inanimate object that comes to life. Everything that happens in the story should revolve around and affect the main character in some way.

- The reader wants to care about and cheer for the main character.
- The reader wants to identify with the character's dreams, habits, or choices.
- All characters need to be human-like, believable, convincing, and interesting.
- The behavior of the characters should also be reasonable for their age and background.
- The main character should grow and learn from mistakes, solve his or her problem, overcome a challenge, make discoveries, and develop over time as people do in real life.

In the book *Come Along, Daisy,* by Jane Simmons, mama duck encourages baby duck to come along, but baby duck wanders off, gets lost, sees frightening things, and eventually finds her way back to her mother. Who can't relate to that story? Certainly, a lot of little kids.

In the book, *No David*, by David Shannon, a little boy is constantly causing trouble in and around his home. He eventually learns that his mother loves him no matter what choices he makes.

Supporting characters are characters that are not the main focus of the story but contribute to the story in a significant way. They can have various personality traits. They can be loyal, kind, funny, crazy, helpful, unsympathetic, mean, or generally disliked by the reader to name a few. Either way, the main character should be reacting to the supporting character's actions and vice versa.

DIVERSITY

Let's talk for a minute about **diversity,** or the inclusion of different types of people. Children want to see characters who remind them of themselves, but our world is a melting pot of people with different ethnicities, languages, beliefs, cultures, and religions. If the story allows for it, make a conscious effort to include characters that are diverse. This could include children who wear glasses, have freckles, have an array of skin colors, have different body shapes and heights, have disabilities or handicaps, speak a foreign language, eat different foods, do things another way, or live differently. Incorporating diverse children helps readers learn acceptance and tolerance. Your book may be the only exposure a child gets to other cultures and ways of life.

STEREOTYPES

A **stereotype** is an idea about how people will act based on the group to which they belong. They are often created about people of specific cultures or races. If you are going to write about a subject, make sure you either know it or have done your research. Almost everyone stereotypes people in some way, without even thinking, but young children are still developing their identity. They shouldn't worry about how the world believes they should think, act, and look. They get enough of that from books, commercials, television shows, games, movies, and believe it or not, their parents.

There are thousands of stereotypes in hundreds of categories.

Here are some examples of **common stereotypes** about genders (boys and girls). Some may be true about boys and girls you know, but they aren't true for ALL boys and girls.

- Boys play with trucks and girls play with dolls.
- Girls wear dresses and boys wear pants.
- Girls watch princess movies and boys watch superhero movies.
- Boys are wild and active, while girls are quiet and passive.
- Boys take more risks than girls.
- Girls wear their hair long, and boys cut theirs short.
- Boys never cry. Girls get emotional.
- Boys are messy and women are clean.
- Only girls paint their nails.
- Boys play with boys and girls play with girls.
- Girls worry about how they look, and boys don't.
- Boys don't wear pink.
- Girls are not good at sports.
- Dad supports the family, and mom takes care of the kids.

Children learn from the roles they see boys and girls play at home, in books, in film, and in other media to which they are exposed. Look at your illustration with an eye toward portraying girls and boys in ways that encourage them to be who they want to be. Can you change the gender of a character from a boy to a girl or vice-versa, without it affecting your story? If you can, then do so. We illustrated a girl riding the skateboard on this page, instead of a boy, because it is considered atypical.

Be careful of cultural stereotypes, as well. People from one culture often categorize people from another culture. Beliefs like African Americans are poor, only Asians stir fry, or all Native Americans wear animal skins are formed out of ignorance.

The SETTING

You can't write a story that happens nowhere. The **setting** is the place or type of surroundings where the story takes place. It will determine the illustration, so the artwork should provide visual cues for the reader. Since young children experience their world differently than adults, they require settings to which they can relate. Children relate things to their personal experiences. Start with the familiar and expand their relationship to the world. The illustration is supposed to show the reader the setting; you shouldn't have to describe it in the text. Let the text focus on the action of the story, flow through the events, and drive the dialog.

Kids like places that are recognizable like their home, the park, a carnival, school, sports fields, dance class, a farm, or a movie theater, but you also want to give children new experiences creatively. Taking children out of the space they know will make the book much more entertaining.

Where the Wild Things Are, by Maurice Sendak, takes a boy out of the house for a wild, fantastical visit with the wild things, then brings him back to the comfort and security of home.

If You Give a Mouse a Cookie, by Laura Numeroff, uses the home differently by introducing an adorable stubborn little mouse who takes a boy through a sequence of events.

The Dialog

A story benefits from having **dialog**, or a conversation between two people. Stories without dialog can be very dull. Readers love listening in on other people's conversations. Put words into the mouths of your characters that sound real and are the way children talk and think. The dialog should make sense and be consistent with what the characters would typically say. For example, a typical 4-year-old would not be able to describe his rocket in scientific terms. The dialog can also reveal information that the reader didn't know. Read your story to friends and other children and get their reaction to what is being said.

Authors use all **five senses** to bring the reader into the story. Whatever your character is seeing, hearing, touching, smelling, and tasting, the reader is also. Sight is the most important sense in descriptive writing, but don't leave the others out - ordinary, everyday sounds transport readers into a scene. Smells can trigger emotions and memories just as well.

Here are some examples of writing using the five senses

- *The waft of his cologne stung her eyes.*
- *Her laugh damaged his ears with its high-pitch.*
- *His tattoo coiled in the shape of a striking snake.*
- *The odor of rotten fish on the boat made her gag.*
- *The salty air on the breeze tickled his taste buds.*
- *She almost lost her footing on the slippery grass.*
- *He was still dripping from the downpour.*
- *The zipline snapped like it was about to break.*
- *When she clenched her fists, he took a step back.*
- *He knew he was late when the crickets began to chirp.*
- *His firm handshake nearly broke her bones.*
- *By the fifth bite, she'd lost all feeling in her taste buds.*

The Story Map

A **story map** helps writers organize their thoughts by filling in the elements of a book or story and identifying the story characters, plot, setting, problem, and solution. There are many different types of story maps. Here are three simplified versions for fiction:

Title: _____

Author: _____

Main Characters:

_____

Setting:

_____

Statement of the Problem:

_____

Summary of the Beginning of the Story:

_____

Summary of the Middle of the Story:

_____

Summary of the Ending of the Story:

_____

Statement of the Solution - Directly related to the problem:

_____

Story Theme • Main Idea (What general message is the author telling the reader?):

_____

Story Map

Setting	Main Character
	Supporting Characters

Problem	Title	Events

Solution	Conclusion

25

Story Map

Setting

Characters

Beginning

Middle

End

NONFICTION

Your book is **nonfiction** if it is based in fact, which is the broadest category of literature. Classroom textbooks, autobiographies, memoirs or life-stories, encyclopedias, essays based on research, dictionaries, thesauruses, news or interview articles are all nonfiction. Non-fiction stories are meant to inform, persuade, and if well written, entertain. An autobiography may have a plot, depending upon how detailed the account is.

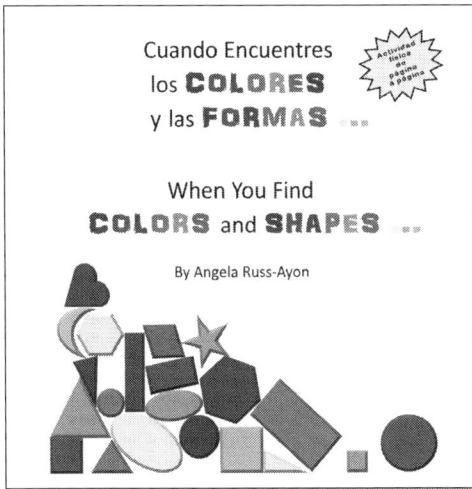

Educational picture books are designed to teach the reader something. This type of book may not have any characters, dialog, or story elements. *When You Find Colors and Shapes*, by Angela Russ-Ayon, is a picture book that encourages children to move as directed every time they locate a shape of a specific color. The goal of the book is to teach young children about shapes and colors, while also getting them up and moving. There is no main character, and there is no plot in the book.

You might see books like these on subjects such as the alphabet, emotions, number sense and math concepts, science, the food pyramid, gardening, cooking, building something, and so forth.

Here are some things to consider if you are writing non-fiction for young children:

- **Content**: The information explores one main subject or topic, and is factual.
- **Conventions**: The writing contains no grammatical errors.
- **Organization**: The writing has a beginning, middle, end, and flows smoothly.
- **Purpose:** The most important thing a reader is supposed to walk away with like new information, a lesson, or a moral of the story.
- **Logical Order:** The facts and research are reasonably or sensibly organized in a way that something would happen.

There are story maps for nonfiction, also. The story maps on the following pages are designed to help nonfiction writers inform or persuade the reader.

Story Map

Subject or Topic

Purpose
Persuade • Inform

Research • Background Information • Details

Examples

Drawings • Diagrams

Conclusion

Story Map

Who?

What?

When?

Where?

Why?

How?

The WORDS in a STORY

People think writing picture books is easy, but it can be challenging. Writing is a skill that gets better with practice. Even the most seasoned writers take classes and workshops to improve their craft, and they write all of the time.

Bait the hook on the first page and imaginatively lead readers through the story. What's the catch? Here are a few examples from popular picture books:

- *The Day the Crayons Quit,* by Drew Dewalt - Children want to keep turning pages to see what the crayons will complain about next.
- *Never, EVER Shout in a Zoo*, by Karma Wilson - The first line warns children not to shout because anything might happen. Of course, they want to see what happens.
- *It's a Book*, by Lane Smith - The first line, "What do you have there?" attracts the reader who wants to hear answers to all of the character's questions.

These are perfect examples of why studying popular children's books can be so helpful when it comes to writing your own.

It's never too late to improve your book when you self-publish by print-on-demand with KDP, but you should revisit, review, edit, and revise your work until you know it is the best it can be before you publish and give the public access to it.

Self-published authors usually write first and illustrate after their stories are complete. Take a closer look at your story. Flip through the illustration and see if it tells your story without any text at all. What is evident in the illustration does not have to be said in words. The illustration and text are supposed to support, but not mirror, each other. If you are saying in words what is obvious to a reader who is looking at the illustration, change the text.

You also want to avoid having the illustration show the opposite of what you have written unless you are creatively writing an entire book about opposites. If you write about how a girl is jumping for joy, then the illustration shouldn't show her sitting down.

Ask yourself if you actually need all of the words you used. Are they interesting? Are they fun to say? Do they add to your story? Can you change them and incorporate the senses? It's okay to teach young children new words and give them a rich language experience. That's how they learn new vocabulary, but they should easily understand most of the words in the book. If there is a list somewhere of words you should use in children's books, it is probably way too long to be helpful to writers.

Don't just write to be writing. Every word in a sentence serves a specific purpose, and every sentence gives a story meaning. Complicated sentence structure is not age-appropriate for pre-readers. Look at how popular the book *Hop on Pop* is from Dr. Seuss, which is filled with simple two and three letter words.

Be conscious of for whom you are writing. Books for babies and toddlers have words that are mostly limited to one or two syllables. They also might have longer words that help younger children identify objects, animals, and insects. Children are introduced to more multi-syllable words as they grow older. Sit and listen to what children say and how they speak. They don't talk like adults.

The **word count** is the total number of words in a book, from the beginning of the story to the end. A picture book for preschoolers might have 150 to 400 words from cover to back, whereas a book for second graders would have a more complex vocabulary with the word count ranging from 500 to 1500. These ranges vary, depending on who you ask. Writing programs like WORD, Google Docs, or PAGES have an option where you can highlight the words and check the word count.

Show the reader how the character feels, by their actions, reactions, gestures, facial expressions, and dialog. No one gets emotional when they read a report about how a character feels. Take a day to observe people. Examine how they react and respond to things. Put yourself in the shoes of the characters and act out the scenes.

Give people **real-life characteristics** and **actions**. Real people hesitate with uncertainty, rush recklessly into trouble, stutter when they're nervous, shiver when it's cold, wipe their foreheads when it's hot, sneeze from allergies, gesture when they celebrate, jerk when startled - and those are just a few actions. There are thousands.

Describe the **feelings** and **emotions** people have in real life. People jump for joy, have nervous tics, zone out under pressure, blush when embarrassed, clench their teeth in anger, have unusual fears, sense something is wrong, shiver with rage, laugh until their cheeks hurt, and cry until they sniffle or hiccup. Characters cry because their happy, sad, or just emotional. They laugh or giggle when something is funny, but also when they're nervous.

Reporting: *"She was scared."*
Showing: *"Her hands trembled as she peaked through her fingers."*

Reporting: *"He was out of shape."*
Showing: *"He heaved and puffed when he climbed the stairs."*

Reporting: *"He was very tired."*
Showing: *"His crutches rubbed him raw and his hands grew numb."*

Instead of using words because they sound cool, use them to describe the **correct actions**. Is the bird swooping or hovering? If it is swooping, it's coming down. If it is hovering, it is hanging in the air. Every word a writer uses helps create a picture in the reader's mind. Are readers seeing what you want them to see?

Young children can be very impressionable. It's best not to encourage them to do something risky, dangerous, or disrespectful. We don't want children jumping off rooftops, skiing off marked paths, skateboarding without helmets, using swear words, or talking back to their grandmother. Parents don't want to encourage that type of behavior, and they are the ones buying books.

Look over your work and see if you have **repeated words**. Find different ways to say things. You have 30 pages or less, and with over 170,000 words in a typical English Dictionary, you shouldn't have to repeat yourself. There is no reason to use the same words unless doing so adds to the story.

In the picture book *No, David*, author David Shannon repeats the line "No, David" on every page until the very end of the book when David's mother tells her son she still loves him. The illustration and repetition of the phrase "No, David" is the story!

In the picture book *Dinousaurumpus*, the author repeats a phrase after every few pages that encourages readers to get up and stomp around like dinosaurs. Children anxiously await the phrase that gives them permission to stand and act silly.

Finally, your work should be yours and yours alone. Taking someone else's work is called **plagiarism**, and is just like stealing someone's possessions. You can't claim someone else's idea or train of thought as your own, copy someone's work without giving them credit, or use a direct quote or paraphrase without citing the source.

GRAMMAR

Grammar is the set of rules that explains how words change their form and combine with other words in a language. It doesn't matter whether you're writing fiction or nonfiction. No matter how creative you are, there are rules of grammar you must follow when you write, like capitalizing the first word in every sentence, putting punctuation at the end of a sentence, and placing a comma where it should go.
Here are some helpful ways to become a better writer.

- Read, read, and read some more.
- Write all of the time. Practice makes writing better.
- Check out grammar books from the library.
- Build your own personal reference book library.
- Research the most common misspelled words.
- Take a writing workshop.
- Pay attention in English class.
- Do a Google search on a computer.

If you aren't sure about grammar or how to use a particular word, turn to a reference book such as a dictionary or thesaurus. Most computer writing programs have spell checks, and you can use online search engines like Google for assistance. You can also ask a parent, mentor, or teacher, but they aren't the ones writing the book. It is best to do your own homework.

Fee-based computer applications like Grammarly.com will review your work for common mistakes such as omitted commas, fragmented sentences, and apostrophe errors.

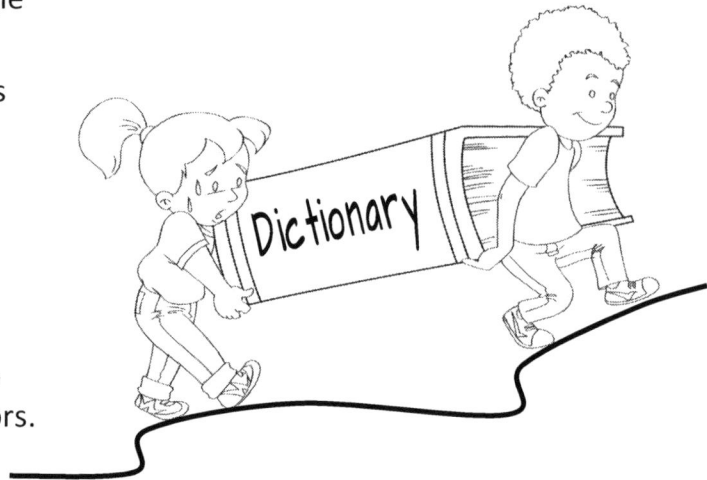

You can also pay a professional **copyeditor**, or line editor, to go through your sentences, story structure, and check details and facts. A **proofreader** corrects typographical errors and grammar mistakes, and may also look for inaccurate facts.

Let's recap:

- Watch your word count.
- Use simple sentence structure for early readers.
- Illustration should not duplicate what is written.
- Illustration should not represent the opposite of what is written.
- Don't report. Show with actions, reactions, facial expressions, gestures, and dialog.
- Describe feelings and emotions in creative ways.
- Give characters real-life traits to which children can relate.
- Use descriptive words correctly, not just because you like them.
- Look out for repeated words. A thesaurus will help you find synonyms.
- Check for grammatical errors and misspelled words.
- Make sure the events in your story are in the right order.
- No plagiarizing.
- Avoid risky, dangerous, or disrespectful storylines.
- Hire a copyeditor or proofreader to check your story.

POINT of VIEW

Keep to one point of view. A **point of view** (POV) is the opinions or feelings of a person involved in your story. The POV is what determines how readers "hear" and "see" what takes place in a story. Once you decide who will tell your story to the reader, stick with that person, or point of view. There are three major kinds of POV.

1. First Person: With this POV, someone is telling the reader his or her story, including thoughts, opinions, emotions, actions, and so on. Telling a story using this POV involves using the pronouns "I" and "we." Here are a few examples.

"I liked to stand in the corner and watch people."

"I will never not ever eat a tomato."

"I am just a little boy. How would I know how to do that?"

"We turned over the timer every time we moved a chess piece."

2. Second Person: With this POV, the reader is invited to participate in the story and learns page-by-page what happens as a result of his or her actions. The author or narrator of the story speaks directly to the reader, telling the reader how to do something. Second person P.O.V. is popular with books that teach, guide, warn, or instruct the reader. This POV involves using the pronoun "you." Here are a few examples.

"If _you_ give a mouse a cookie,…"

"_You_ don't know what you've got, until it's gone."

"To make lemonade, _you_ combine lemon juice, water, and sugar."

"Maybe _you_ should put this book back. _You_ don't want to let the monkeys out."

3. Third Person: With a third person POV, the readers feel like someone is holding a camera and filming the events, or like they are listening to people gossip. Telling the story using this POV involves using pronouns like "he," "she," "it," "they," or a persons name. Here are a few examples.

"_She_ went out through the back door, and that's when she saw it."

"_He_ was an honest young man. That's why _he_ gave the money back."

"_She_ would not tell her little brother how the bad man took the snowman's nose."

"_They_ shared a secret about their new dog and didn't want to tell anyone."

RHYMING

Rhyming is when a word, syllable, or end of a line has the same sound as another. Children's books don't have to rhyme, but if you want your book to rhyme, you should write perfect rhymes, not words that almost rhyme, called **near rhymes.** Near rhymes are very popular in mainstream songs but are not for young children who are still learning read. For example, a perfect rhyme is meat/feet/neat. Both the "ee" sound and the ending "t" sound match perfectly. Similarly, note/boat/tote share both the "oh" sound and the ending "t" sound. However, near rhymes such as note/spoke, or life/dice share the same middle sounds, but not the same endings.

Exact rhymes:
bug, hug, slug
dice, mice, lice
same, name, came
end, friend, send

Near rhymes:
bug, fun, ton
life, dice, tide
same, Jane,
friend, again

Write your story first, then work on the rhyming. One of the best rhymers in the history of children's books was Dr. Seuss, even though he sometimes made up rhyming words that made no sense.

If you read a book out loud, you'll probably be able to notice a rhythm, or a beat, running through it, as you would hear in a song. If the rhyme is off, the phrases will sound awkward, like a hiccup. Rhyming should blend into the story and flow naturally, with a repetitive, measured syllable count. It helps to clap out the syllables of each line to make sure they are steady and consistent.

Whether you rhyme every line, every other line, or even every fourth line, rhyming takes practice. If you decide to use near rhymes, then go that route through your whole book. Don't bounce back and forth. Your book may not rhyme perfectly, but it will sound nice. The story is more important than the rhyme. If your attempts to rhyme are messing up the story, then abandon the rhyming all together.

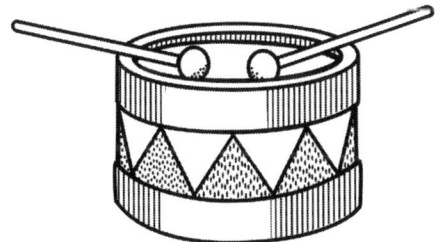

EDITING

When you **edit** a book, you check, correct, modify, and rearrange the work. Editing is the stage of writing when you improve on what you've written and make your story more clear. It requires reading, re-reading, re-reading, re-reading, and re-reading your work. Even the best writers revise their stories multiple times. Editing involves making all different kinds of corrections.

Here are some main issues for which to look:

- Checking for errors in punctuation, grammar, and spelling, including omitted or incorrect use of words.
- Removing unnecessary or inappropriate words.
- Rearranging sentences.
- Modifying scenes.
- Correcting tenses.
- Filling in gaps and holes in the story.
- Making sure the story flows smoothly from one idea to the next.
- Fact-checking things like dates, times, names, historical details, locations, computations, and other details.
- Filling in headlines, headers, photo captions, or summaries.
- Double-checking illustrations, diagrams, or photos.

Step back from your story for a week. When you reread it, read it out loud, checking for one issue at a time. See more "Proofreading" tips on page 92.

Here are a few helpful tips:

- Ask family, friends, and adults who you respect to review your work.
- Be willing to listen to positive, helpful, constructive criticism.
- Take command of your story and make any changes that make sense and will improve your book.
- Ignore the opinions of people who are negative or who discourage you from writing.

The ILLUSTRATION

An **illustration** is artwork or a picture used to clarify something or provide an example. Picture books earned their name because of the fun, lush, unique, and captivating illustration that helps tell each story. It's the illustration that grabs the interest of children and keeps them wanting to turn to the next page.

If you are going to self-publish a picture book, you have three options:

- illustrate your book
- get someone else to illustrate for free
- buy images from a photo or illustration provider
- pay someone to illustrate your story

If you illustrate your book, develop your own unique style. It wouldn't hurt to take a few art classes or read books on how to draw.

You cannot just use any artwork or clip art you find on the internet. Nor can you take an image you find in a Google search, or scan an image you like from another book or magazine. That is called **copyright infringement**. Someone else owns that work, and you can't use another person's artwork without asking permission or paying for the right to use it if you plan to sell your book. Unless you find an image that is **commercial-free** or **copyright-free**, you can't use any image in a book that you plan to sell on Amazon KDP or anywhere else.

Commercial free means the image can be used to market the book, promote the book, or sell the book to make or try to make money. **Public domain** images are also free for public use and are not subject to copyright, which means you can do what you want with them. The only issue with using random images you find on the internet is that the artwork in the book won't look as if one person did all of the pictures.

Even if you obtain the right to use artwork, any image you use for printing or publishing has to be at a hi-resolution meant for "High Quality" or "Commercial Press," which is 300 dpi or higher. A lot of what you find on the internet is not the proper resolution for quality printing.

If you choose someone else to illustrate, pick someone who has a style you like and uses a **medium** (or way of completing the artwork) you prefer such as watercolors, colored pencils, acrylic paint, crayons, ink or pencil, or pastels. Most artists specialize in only one or two mediums, and that's how they do their best work.

Select an **artistic style** and medium, and stick to it. You want your artwork to be consistent throughout your book. For example, your book won't look uniform if some pages are watercolor, and others are crayon drawings. Your color images should have the same style and appearance as if they were all done by the same illustrator.

There are different ways to finish the illustration. Artists produce artwork on tablets using drawing programs, directly on a computer using illustration software, or on paper or canvas that will eventually be scanned. Amazon KDP prints from digital files, so the artwork has to be digital, too. In other words, no matter how the illustration is completed, it has to be eventually uploaded from a computer.

Inspiration is everywhere. Look through other picture books, magazines, websites, social media, television, movies, trending articles, and be aware of everything and everyone around you.

Writers visualize how they want their illustration to look, like a movie playing in their heads. Draw and sketch until you end up with what you think you want, even if it's only to give an artist an idea of what you want. Just keep in mind that if someone else illustrates your story, the artwork may not come out like you pictured it in your head.

Begin the artwork by sketching out your ideas using simple drawings. Even stick figure drawings are okay. Sketch out each page and arrange the pages in order, building a storyboard. A **storyboard** is an easy way to organize your story using small rough illustrations in sequence. Read your storyboard out loud to see how the text and illustration flows. You might find you need to rearrange, delete, or modify the story, illustrations, or sequence of pages. Storyboards are provided at the end of this book.

Leave plenty of room for the text, or it will have to be placed over important features in the illustration.

The fun is in the details! Mix things up! Since books are read again and again, it's nice to provide the reader with layers of illustrated detail. Plan your artwork in such a way that if the book is read more than once, and it usually is, readers have something new to discover. Give them something they didn't see the last time they read the book, such as various insects or animals, an image in the picture hanging on the wall, toys in the playroom, a hidden face, food in the open refrigerator, or labels and signs.

Young children are still learning about everything: colors, sizes, numbers, the alphabet, objects, and living things. No matter what the ocean story is about below, this picture gives parents and children a lot to talk about and identify. Children can count fish, recognize fish, compare characteristics of fish, and so forth.

Text goes here.

A book also flows much better if the illustrated pages have changes in perspective. **Perspective** is the way readers see and experience the events and feelings in a story. In art, it's a way of drawing objects to give the reader a particular view. You can do this in a few different ways, but the most common for picture books are:

- go from busy with a lot of activity to idle with nothing much happening.

- go from loud images with a lot of detail to quiet images with not much at all.

- change the viewpoint—go from far away to close up, overhead, or from behind, giving the readers scenes from different angles.

Here is an example of two different viewpoints. One displays blueberries close up, and the other has an entire blueberry bush and character from far away. They are placed opposite of each other in the story.

You don't have to switch back and forth from one perspective to another, but doing so makes the book more visually appealing. That said, a common mistake is to try to do too much when less does the job. Any illustration that is too busy distracts readers because they will have no idea where to look, or bores readers with repetitive imagery.

Pay close attention to your **color palette**, or range of colors. A color palette might include earth tones such as brown, burgundy, cream, and dark green. Maybe you like bright, bold colors like crimson red, ocean blue, hot pink, and sunshine yellow. Whatever colors you choose, you want them to flow harmoniously through the pages like the steady beat of a song. Think of it this way, if the pages of your book all came apart, would someone be able to easily put your book back together because of your use of color, tone, and artistic style?

Specific colors have meanings and **moods**. Dull, drab colors often symbolize sadness, anger, or exhaustion. Bright colors embody happiness or excitement, red is often used for anger, and dark colors make people feel scared.

Show, don't tell. The pictures are supposed to tell the story and support the text, not repeat what you just said in words. If you have written something that is obvious in the picture, either delete those lines or change the illustration because the reader can already see what you wrote.

Keep important features and images away from the **inside margins**. If you run a face across the spread of the book, you will lose some of the facial detail in the gutter, like this girl's nose.

Place essential images and features away from the **outside margins** where they can be cut off. Be aware of the safe area, which is at least one-half inch from the margins all around, for good measure. You don't want to lose parts of faces and interesting things children will want to see.

People read from left to right, so the illustration should flow the same way, like cars all moving in the same direction. Turning characters toward the right if they are facing left makes for a more comfortable read.

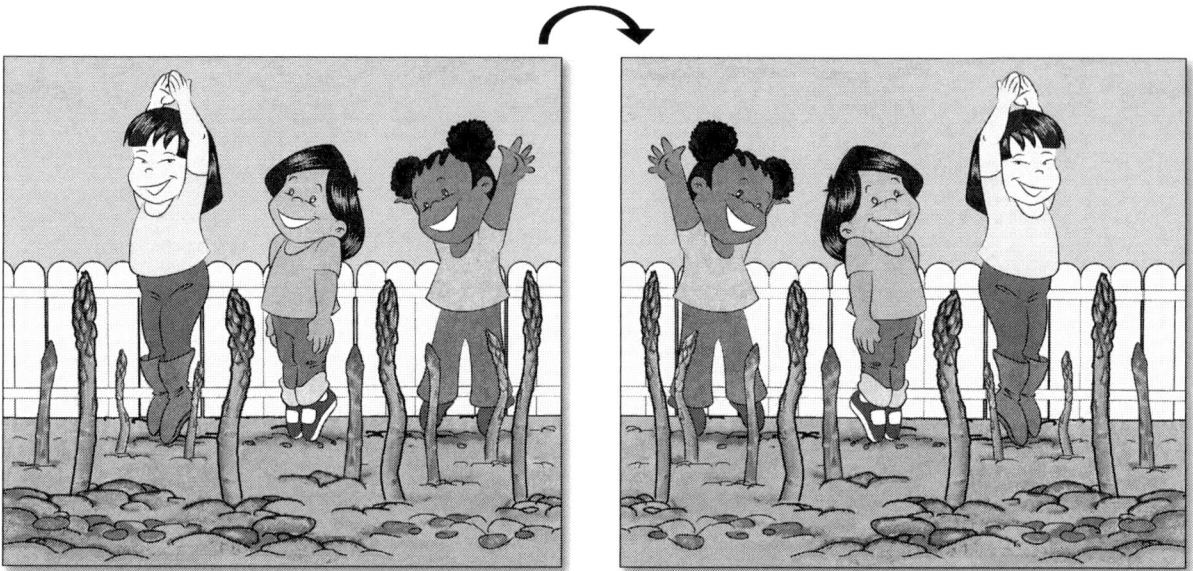

Give illustrations a human element using the entire body or body parts. You want children to walk a few minutes in the same shoes as the characters in your story. Have you ever watched children play? One child isn't interested in a toy until another child picks it up. You want the reader interested in picking up that toy, too. Do you see the difference between the two images below? How do you think children will feel when they see the image on the right?

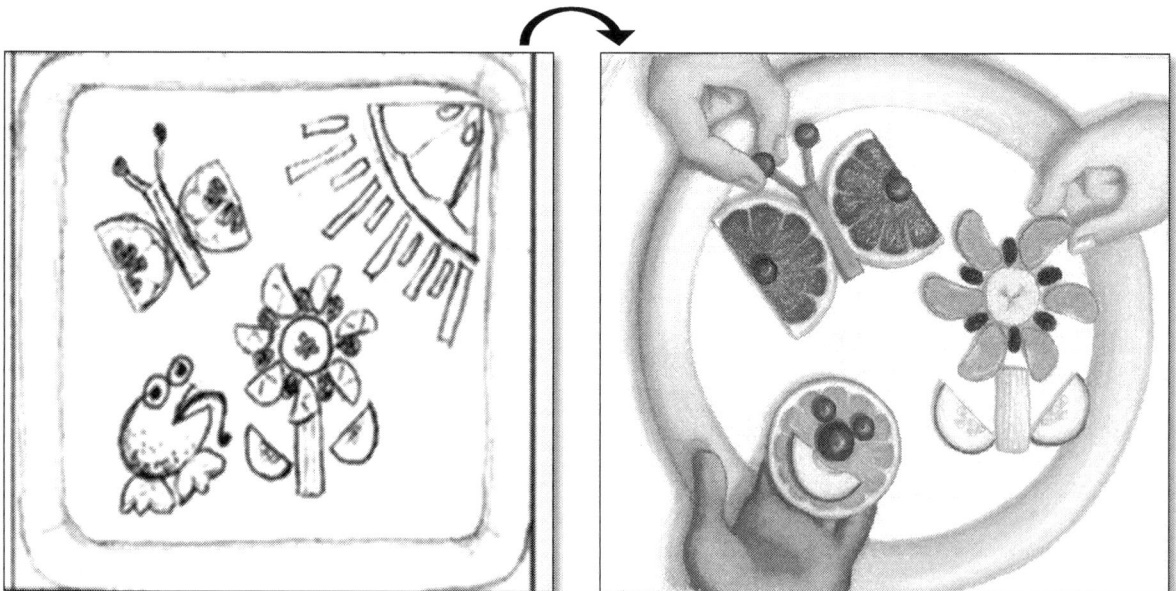

Sometimes there are obvious problems with a story or illustration that the author or illustrator doesn't see until someone points them out. Ask a friend or mentor to look at your work and see if there is anything you missed. Be receptive and open to ideas that will improve your book.

Let's review! Your story is written.

1. Decide who will illustrate your picture book.
2. Do not use someone else's artwork without permission.
3. Begin the illustration with rough sketches.
4. Don't forget to leave room for the text.
5. Build a storyboard, laying out the illustration in sequence.
6. Revise, rewrite, and rearrange your work.
7. Revisit your text to see if the illustration supports it.
8. Select an artistic style and stick with it.
9. Choose a medium and stick with it.
10. Be consistent with your color palette.
11. Tell your story from different illustrated perspectives.
12. Keep important images and features away from the margins, and out of the gutter.
13. Place images with action flowing to the right.
14. Make the illustration touchy, feely with human elements.
15. Ask a friend, family member, or mentor to review your work.
16. Join a writer's critique group for feedback.

The PARTS of a BOOK

The **cover** of a book is the thick protective outer part on the front that displays the title, an image that will attract a buyer, and the name of the author and illustrator. Paperback books, also known as "soft covers," have a wraparound cover that is rigid, laminated cardstock. Cardstock is stiffer than the paper used for the interior pages, and it's flexible.

Here are some samples of book covers. Design your own cover or create a cover using KDP's Cover Creator tool which supplies free stock images you can use.

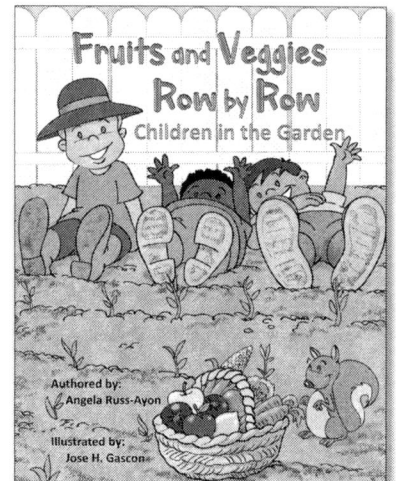

The **back** of a book is the thick protective outer part you see when you flip over the book. It includes a written description summarizing the book. People usually pick up a book because of the cover and then turn it over to see what it's about on the back. A well-written description draws the buyer in, and if the buyer is still interested, he or she might start flipping through pages to investigate further.

Along with the description, a barcode is placed on the back of the book. It identifies the International Standard Book Number (ISBN), and sometimes the price, but we will go over that later.

Here are a few examples of the backs of books. You don't have to put artwork on the back of a book, but it does make the book more appealing, as you can see.

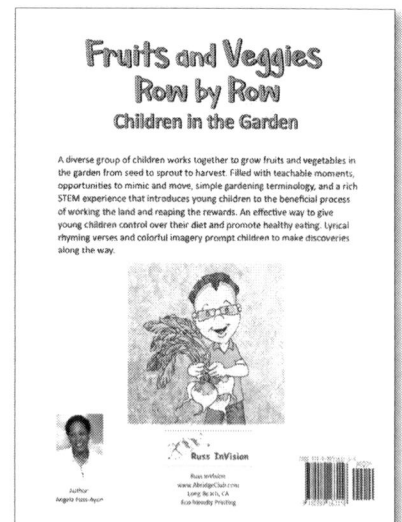

The PARTS of a BOOK

Interior Pages

Back

Cover

Spine

The cover and back of a book are connected at the spine. The **spine** of a book is the outside edge where the pages are gathered and bound. It secures the pages and acts as a hinge that allows the book to open and close without losing the pages. Typically, the spine is the first part of a book people see when it's sitting on a shelf. Some books are not thick enough to print text on the spine. The words would be too small to read and the printing could shift when the book is trimmed and bound. **KDP recommends that you not print on the spine of books under 100 pages.**

The cover can be printed with either a **glossy** and shiny, or **matte** and flat finish. Both are nice, but a shiny finish doesn't show as many fingerprints and scratches as a matte finish. On glossy covers, the color black shows darker and artwork is more striking. Glossy is pretty standard for textbooks, children's books, and novels.

The cover and back of the book can be printed in full color or black and white. It is up to you. There is no additional cost for Amazon KDP to print the cover in color, even if the interior pages are black and white.

When Amazon KDP's team refers to the **interior pages,** they are talking about the pages you turn on the inside of the book. In the publishing industry, each interior page is called a **leaf,** and the pages combined are known as the **text block.**

The **gutter** is the inside margin of a bound book.

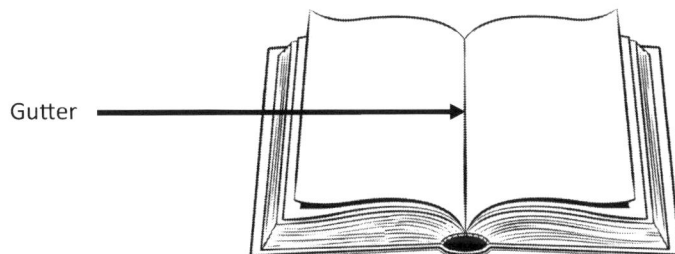

Gutter

The INTERIOR PAGES

The **interior pages** of your book can be black and white, or color. Picture books are usually color. You can't save money by reducing the number of color interior pages you have. You can print 29 pages in black and white and one page in color, but if you want to include just one color image in the interior, the entire interior of the book has to be printed in color. It costs more to print paperbacks in color than if you print them in black and white.

Reminder! **At KDP, the cover of the book is printed in full color; front and the back.**

Paper Color: Amazon KDP allows you to print on white or cream paper if you have black and white interior pages, but it limits you to white paper for color interiors to give you the best contrast between the printed text, the artwork, and the background of the page. For color books, white paper makes the pages easier to read. Besides, if you print color on cream, the colors won't come out as crisp and clear.

The **weight** of the **paper** refers to the thickness of a book's paper stock. If you feel the cover of a paperback book and then touch the interior pages of the same book, you will feel a difference in the thickness or weight of the paper. Print-on-demand (POD) paperweight can range from about 50 to 70 pounds. **Amazon KDP does not give you a choice of paper weight.** They offer standard paper weights for black and white or color books that are always subject to change. You do get a choice of paper weight when you choose a professional offset printer who prints large quantities of books, but the difference in paper weight will affect your cost to print.

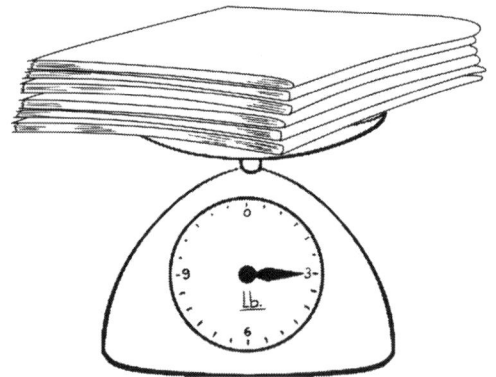

The PAGE COUNT

The **page count** is the number of pages in the interior of a book. Most picture books have 32 interior pages, but they don't have to. They can have 24, 28, 32 or more. **Amazon KDP will not bind a book with less than 24 pages.**

Why are picture books 32-pages? The reason is that 32 is the perfect number of pages for a printer to print on the front and back of one large sheet of paper without wasting paper or using another sheet, saving you and the printer money. Thirty-two pages is also a good book length for young children and their parents to read: not too long and not to short.

You cannot actually use all 32-pages for your story and illustration in a picture book. One page is used as a title page, and another is used as a copyright page (called the **front matter**), so in a 32-page book, you will only be able to use a maximum of 30 pages or less for your story. However, you do not have to use all 30 pages.

If you tell KDP that you are publishing a 32-page book, but you only have 29 illustrated pages, plus a title and copyright page, then one page will be left blank at the beginning or end of your finished book. If you have 28 illustrated pages, then two pages will be left blank at the end, and so on. Either way, the book will still have 32 pages.

You also have the option of telling KDP that you are publishing a 28-page book. It's up to you. If you do, you will only have 26 pages available for illustration, because you will still lose the title and copyright pages. Browse through a few picture books and see how they are laid out.

LAYING OUT a BOOK

Once the story is written, it's time to plan how the illustration will be laid out. When you **layout** your book, you arrange the text, images, pages, and other objects. Use storyboards to assist you.

Here is an example of using all 32 interior pages of a 32-page picture book. The first two pages are reserved for the title and copyright © pages. Here is an example of how the interior pages would look. You upload every interior page in order and in one PDF file to KDP, beginning with the title and copyright pages.

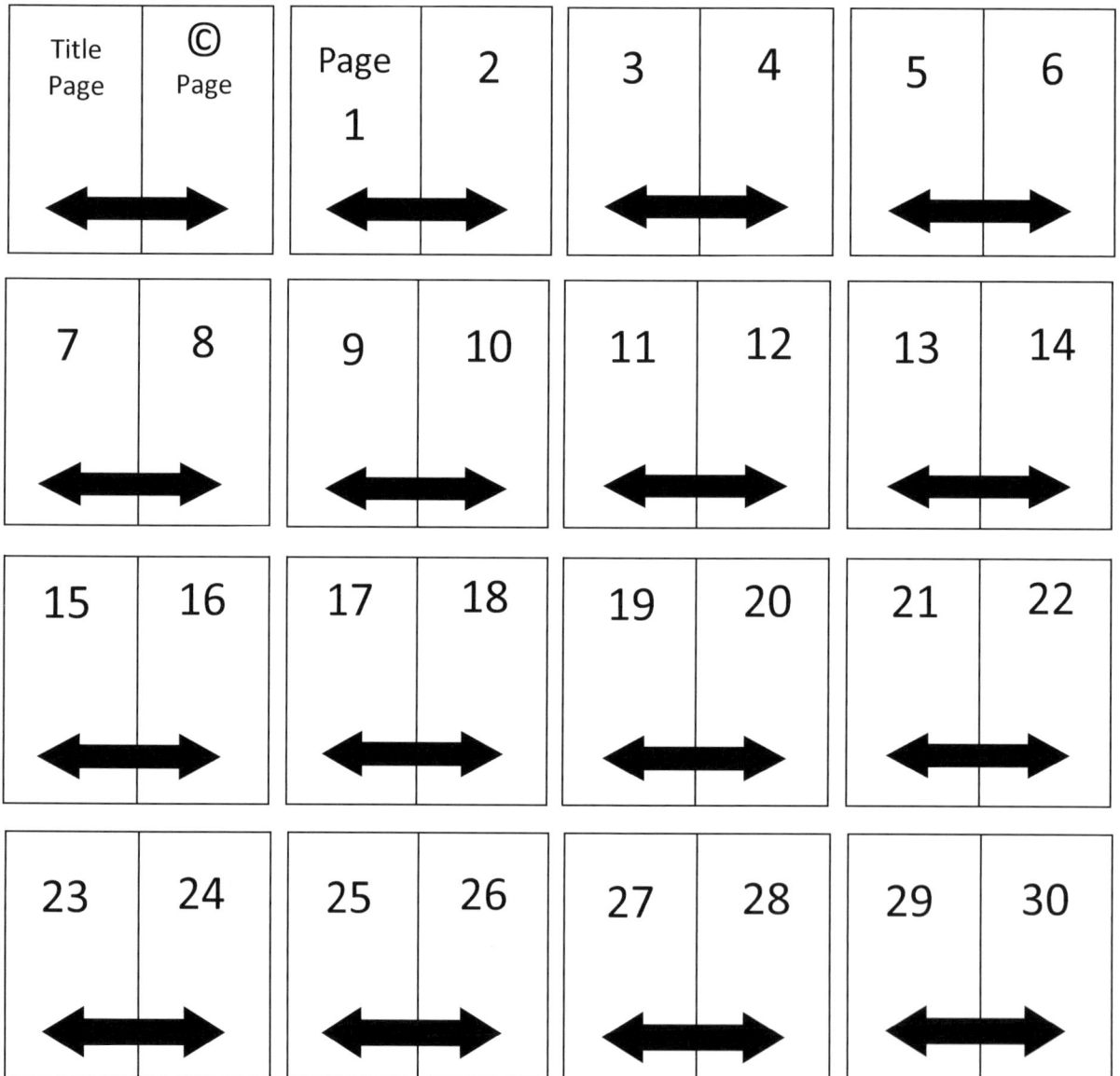

Title Page	© Page	Page 1	2	3	4	5	6
← →		← →		← →		← →	

7	8	9	10	11	12	13	14
← →		← →		← →		← →	

15	16	17	18	19	20	21	22
← →		← →		← →		← →	

23	24	25	26	27	28	29	30
← →		← →		← →		← →	

LAYING OUT a BOOK

Here is an example of what the interior page layout of a book will look like if you are only using 28 interior illustrated pages of a 32-page picture book. Again, the first two pages are reserved for the title and copyright © pages. You tell KDP that you are publishing a 32-page picture book and upload 30 interior pages total, including the title page and copyright page in order and in one PDF file. The two pages will be left blank when KDP assembles the book.

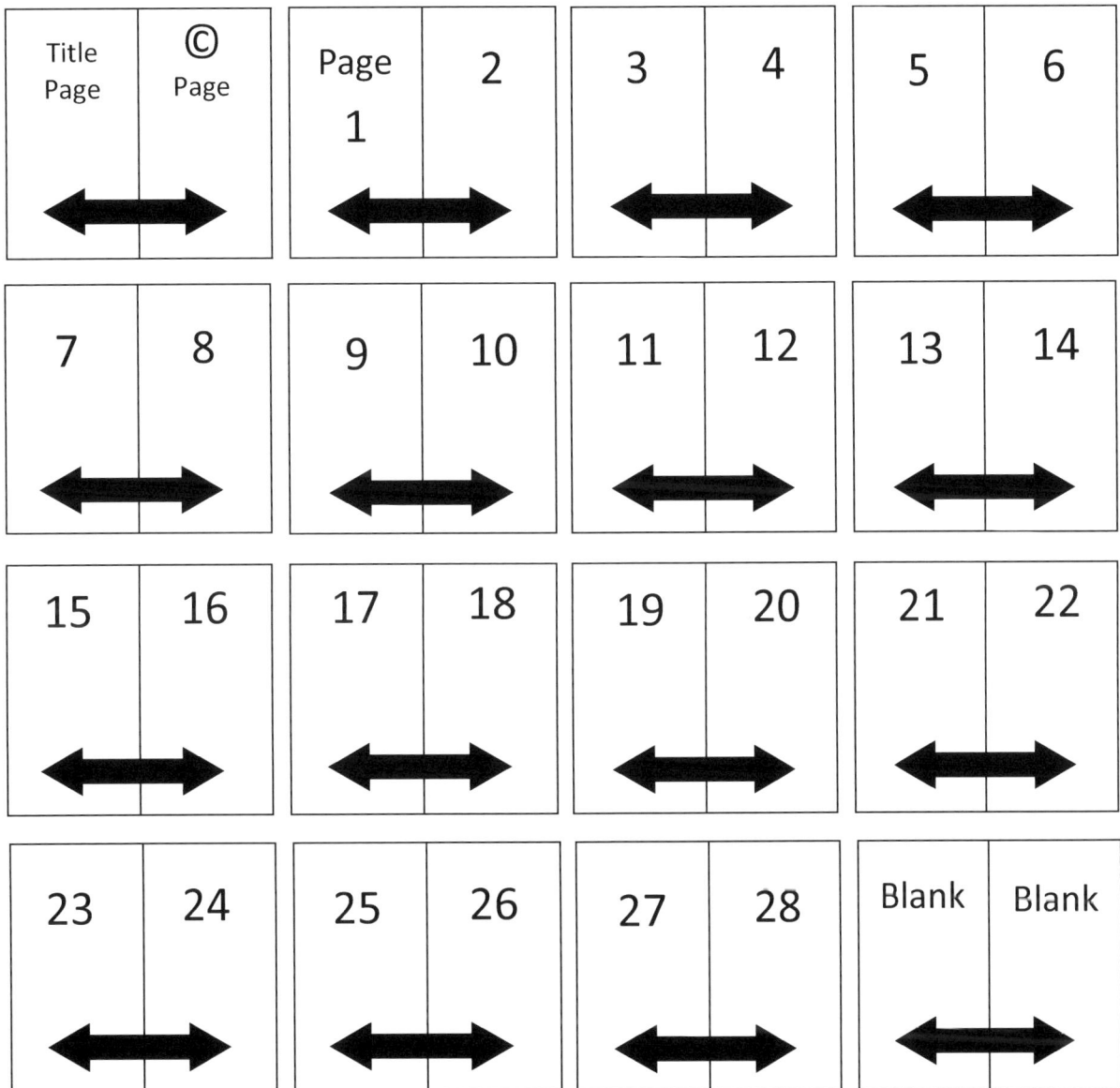

Title Page / © Page ←→	Page 1 / 2 ←→	3 / 4 ←→	5 / 6 ←→
7 / 8 ←→	9 / 10 ←→	11 / 12 ←→	13 / 14 ←→
15 / 16 ←→	17 / 18 ←→	19 / 20 ←→	21 / 22 ←→
23 / 24 ←→	25 / 26 ←→	27 / 28 ←→	Blank / Blank ←→

The BLANK PAGES

It is perfectly okay to end up with one to four blank pages in your book, but you can find a way to make the blank pages useful. Here are some options for making good use of them:

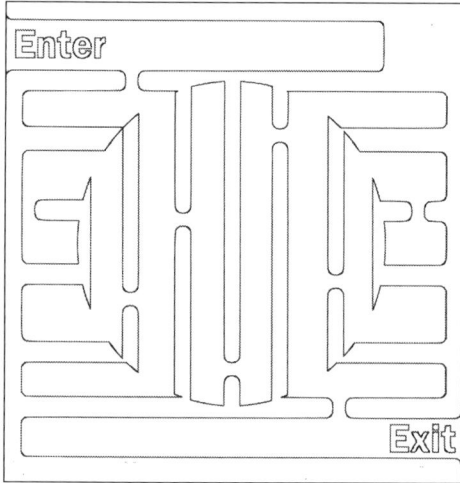

- table of contents
- a glossary of terms
- instructions and diagrams
- paper crafts (origami or paper plane)
- coloring pages
- recipes
- mazes and puzzles
- games (number, words, shapes)
- images for retelling or restructuring the story
- fast facts about the subject of your story
- a family tree
- a map
- lyrics and/or sheet music
- handmade puppet instructions
- details and background information
- teachable moments
- a history lesson

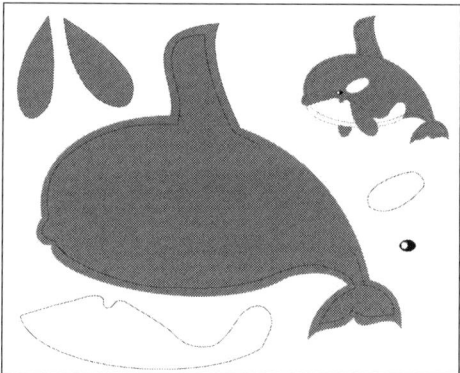

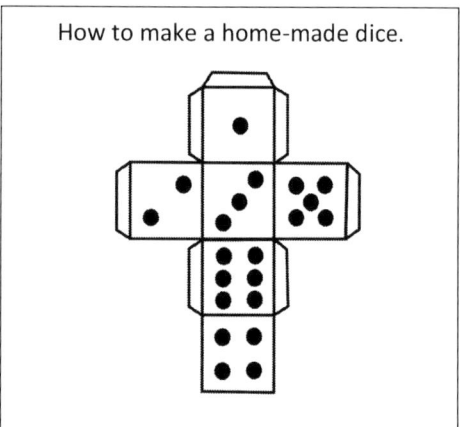

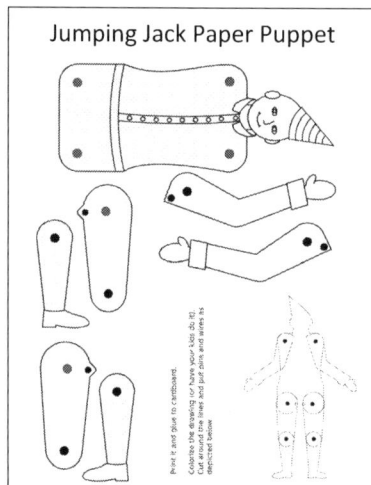

How to make a home-made dice.

Jumping Jack Paper Puppet

Die Gedanken sind frei

The SET-UP

When you self-publish, you don't have to photocopy and submit a manuscript for anyone to review, but you do have to prepare your finished story and set-up the illustration for uploading on the computer. **Uploading** is the process of publishing on the Internet. On a self-publishing platform like KDP, your book has to be prepared and uploaded as if it is ready to be pulled from a shelf, with a single cover and back file, and another file with the interior pages in order.

KDP will also accept other formats for publishing a downloadable e-book.

If you don't want to self-publish, and you decide to mail your story to a traditional publisher, your manuscript must be typed and properly formatted. In most cases, there is no need to send artwork. Publishers like to assign illustrators to their stories. *The Writer's Market* has contact and submission information to help writers get their manuscripts published. Again, once your book is finished and your manuscript has been submitted, you sit back and wait for a response. Be patient. This process can take three to twelve months. Editors have stacks and stacks of books to review, with more being delivered every day.

A **spread** is a general description for a pair of facing pages, typically the left- and right-hand pages. An easy way to understand this is by opening a book and press it flat against a table so the book is spread out.

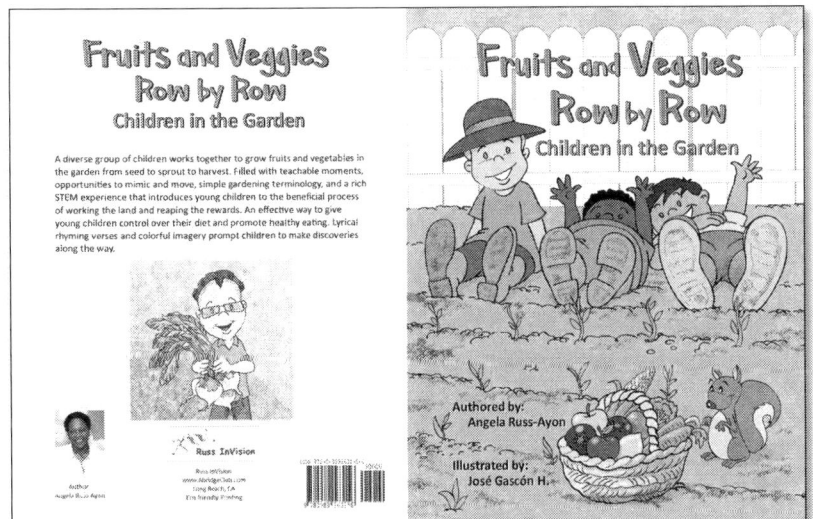

UPLOADING the COVER and BACK

If you are self-publishing with Amazon KDP, you upload the cover, spine, and back of the book to the KDP website as a spread as you see below. KDP will accept a PDF file that is saved at a resolution meant for "High Quality" or "Commercial Press" (300 dpi or higher) printing. Cover files larger than 650MB won't convert. They recommend a file size of 40MB or less because files that are too large can slow down printing.

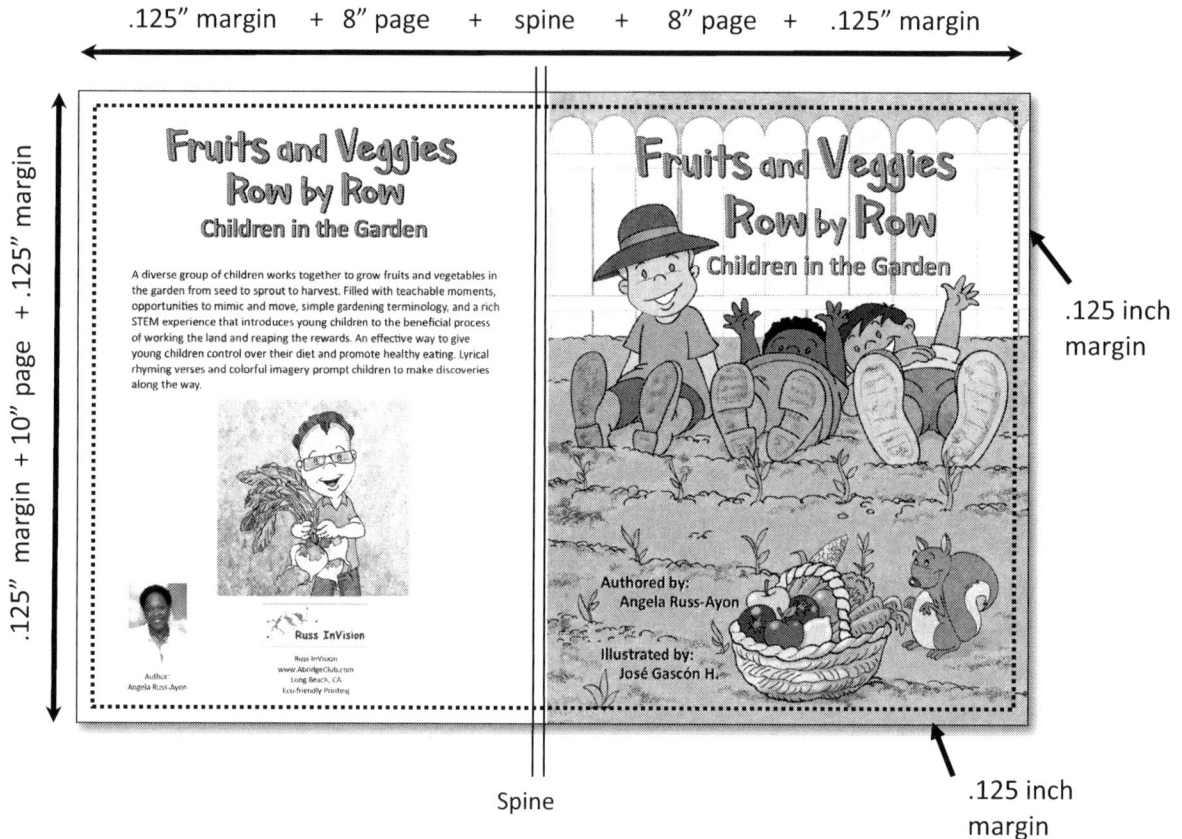

.125" margin + 8" page + spine + 8" page + .125" margin

.125" margin + 10" page + .125" margin

.125 inch margin

.125 inch margin

Spine

You must upload a single PDF file of the spread online with KDP, which includes the back cover, spine, and front as one image.

Set the size of the page spread to include a .125 inch (⅛") margin all around. Plus an additional measurement for the spine, which is determined by the number of interior pages in the book. The number of interior pages will determine how thick the book will be. KDP offers a template or a calculator online to assist you, but the spine equals the number of pages times .002252.

The **bleed** is printing that goes beyond the edge of where the pages are trimmed. The bleed ends up being the area that is trimmed off when the pages are cut from the printer's big sheet, and it gives the printer a small amount of leeway for the paper shifting and human error. When adding images, make sure they extend 0.125" (3 mm) past the final trim size on all edges. This will prevent a white border from appearing at the edge when your book is trimmed.

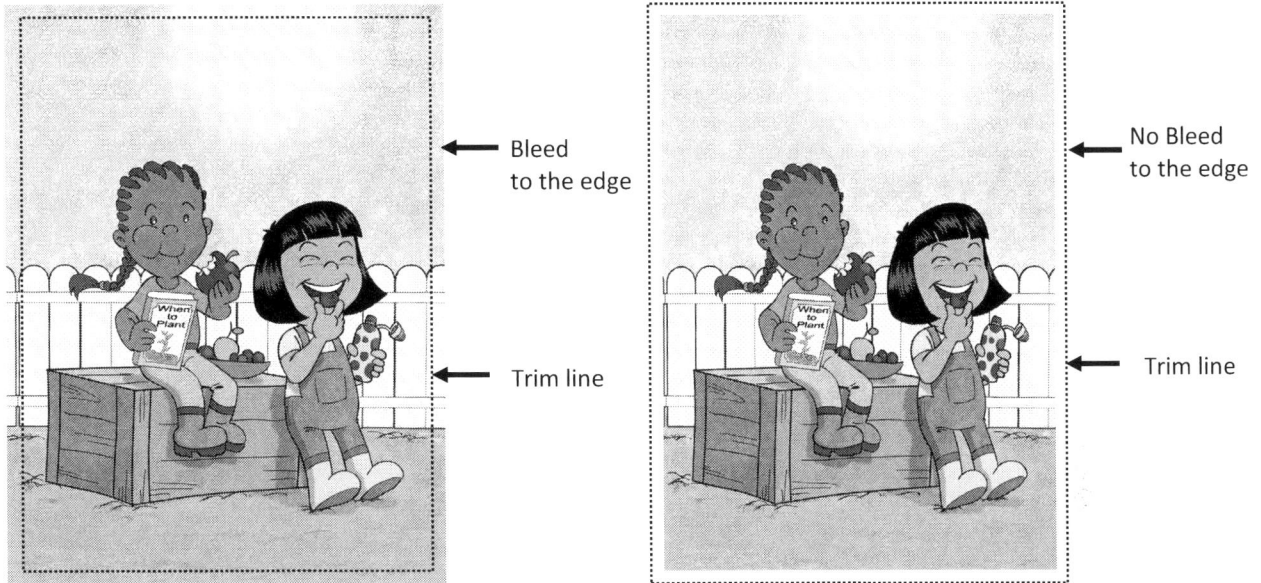

Bleed
to the edge

Trim line

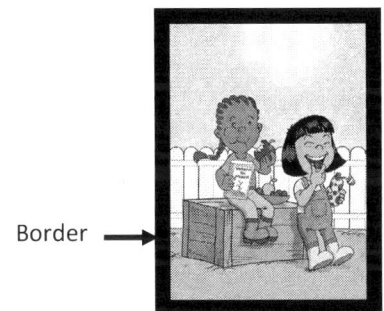

No Bleed
to the edge

Trim line

Borders around the pages are not recommended because when the printer trims the pages, it might cut them uneven. If this happens, the pages will look like they are sitting a little sideways.

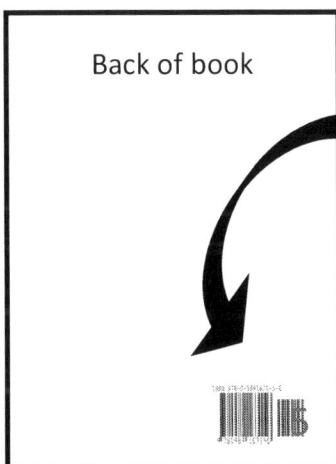

Border

Back of book

The information that appears on the cover of your book has to match the information you enter when you set-up the book online with KDP. All of the book's details have to match what the KDP reviewers will see, including the title, subtitle, author's name, illustrator's name, edition, and ISBN. If the information on the cover of your book doesn't match what you type on the online submission, the book will not pass the review process.

PAPERBACK vs. HARDBACK

Amazon KDP takes the choice of paperback vs. hardback right out of your hands. They don't print hardback books.

Paperback, or softcover books, are books with covers made out of heavy paper stock. They are less expensive to print and lighter to ship than hardcover books. **Hardback**, or hardbound books, have covers made out of heavy cardboard, cloth, or leather, so they last longer than paperback books and weigh more, as well. There are other printers in the self-publishing market that print hardback books, but hardbacks can be costly for you to print and for readers to purchase.

The BINDING

Binding is the act of fastening the individual sheets, or interior pages, of a book together.

Paperback books can be bound in different ways to secure the pages to the spine. Amazon KDP uses **perfect binding**, which is the kind of binding you see on most paperback and hardback books. The pages and cover are glued together at the spine. You can't remove pages that are perfect bound like you can in a loose-leaf binder. The finished paperback books are easy to stack, don't weigh as much as hardback books, and look very professional.

Other popular bindings are available in the paperback printing industry, but not from KDP.

Saddle-stitching is a term that sounds misleading. It is a method of binding loose-leaf pages of a paperback book using staples down the middle or the gutter. It is an inexpensive way of binding and is commonly seen in Scholastic Book Club books, but **KDP does not bind this way**.

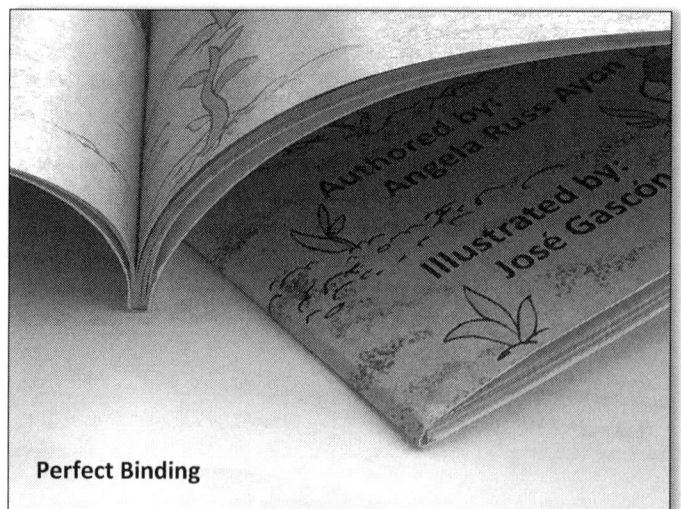

Perfect Binding

Coil binding is when a single spiraled piece of wire or plastic is wound through holes at the edges of loose-leaf pages. The book is sturdy and looks presentable, but this type of binding can cost more money. It is mostly used for business proposals, school notebooks, or presentations. **KDP does not publish coil-bound books.**

Adhesive casebound is the standard binding option for **hardcover books**. This binding method protects the interior pages with a hardcover. People purchase hardback books if they want to have them for a long time since the covers are difficult to tear. **KDP does not print hardback books at this time.** There is nothing stopping you from finding a source that will print your book as a hardback with a different ISBN, but expect to pay more for this type of binding and for having two different versions of your book.

If you want to write for babies, who don't know any better than to eat the pages of a book, then **board books** are recommended. Board books are unique in that every page is super thick cardboard that is almost impossible to bend. They are a toy as much as they are a book. The two-page spreads are printed, then cut, assembled, and glued together by hand, one set of pages at a time. **KDP does not print board books.**

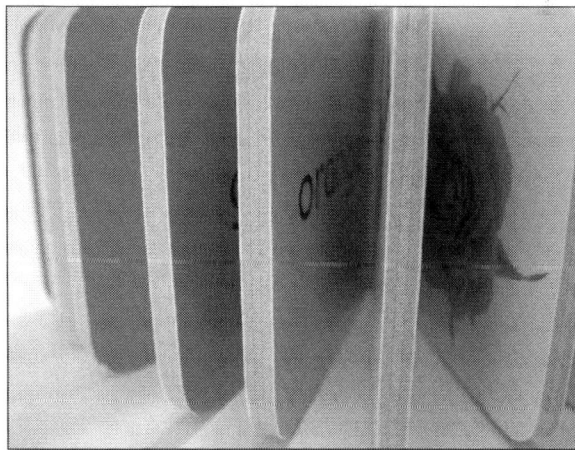

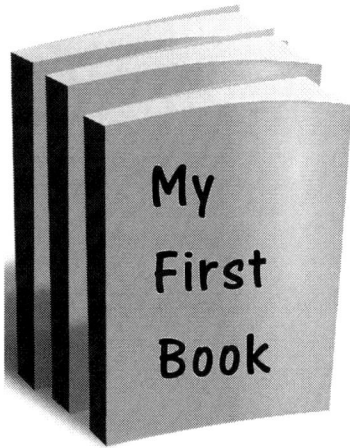

PRINTING-ON-DEMAND

Print-on-demand (POD) is a way of digitally printing books only as you need them, or after they are purchased. The books are printed from a digital file, such as a PDF. On KDP, you can also upload a DOC (.doc), DOCX (.docx), HTML (.html), or RTF (.rtf). Instead of printing a large quantity, like 2,000 copies at a time, POD offers the option of printing as many books as you need.

POD books can be ordered for readings, autograph sessions, book fairs, conventions, or sharing with family and friends for very little investment. POD books give authors a chance to test the market and see how well their book will be received. As a print-on-demand publisher, Amazon Kindle Direct Publishing (KDP) makes books available to markets around the world without the author or illustrator having to worry about selling, shipping, storage, and distribution, but there are other print-on-demand services out there.

POD books can be made available to buyers quickly, usually within a week of uploading and approving files. Another benefit of POD is that the cover and interior pages of a book can be updated or changed between print runs. To make changes, you upload new files which are reviewed again by Amazon KDP and re-published under the same International Standard Book Number (ISBN).

You cannot, however, change the type of binding, number of pages, book size, title, author's name, or language of the book without changing the ISBN and uploading an entirely new version of the book. Books with unique features like pop-ups, cut-outs, inserts, page folds, and the like are not a good fit for POD. They are considered custom books that require printers with special equipment.

If you need a large quantity and would like to save some money, print-ready files can always be taken to a commercial offset printer who can print 2,000 copies or more.

This book focuses on self-publishing a printed picture book that a person can touch, feel, and page turn using Amazon KDP, but you can also publish your picture book on KDP as a Kindle e-book.

E-Books

E-books are downloadable books that can be read on devices such as tablets, phones, and computers from top e-book retailers such as Amazon Kindle, Apple, Barnes & Noble's Nook, and Kobo. **Amazon KDP only publishes digital books to Kindle** at this time, but there are other services that publish to multiple platforms.

Some readers are e-book fanatics and only read downloaded books, so it's good to publish your book in print as well as downloadable versions. The process of self-publishing an e-book and a print book is slightly different.

You will most likely need to take your illustrated manuscript and prepare it for publication in different ways if you want to publish various downloadable e-books versions.

Getting your printed picture book converted to a KDP Kindle e-book is a quick process, but it takes a learning curve and some trial and error. A Kindle e-book, like all others, has to be published in a machine-readable format for tablets and e-book readers. Amazon KDP lets you upload and convert your e-book manuscript using several supported file formats, such as WORD docx, HTML, MOBI, ePUB, and others. PDFs do not produce good results as e-books. KDP encourages you to review your book before you hit the "PUBLISH" button. It is up to you to proofread your book and make sure it looks good on different devices by using free preview tools such as Calibre (https://calibre-ebook.com).

You can't specify certain details with an e-book such as the font size because the person reading the e-book can change the size of the font on their e-Reader to whatever size they want. In the case of most picture books, the text on pages is embedded in the picture. In other words, the text and illustrations on the interior pages are one image, whereas the text on the Publisher's Page and description on the back of the book can stand alone. It's the stand-alone text that allows readers to search for keywords and content that is in a book.

The PRINT RUN

The cost of printing paperback picture books that someone can hold in their hands depends mostly on the trim size of the book, the number of interior pages, the paper quality and weight, the binding, whether the interior pages are color or black and white, and the quantity printed in the print run.

A **print run** is the number of copies of a book, magazine, pamphlet, etc. that is printed at one time. It doesn't matter if you order 2 or 200 books to be printed. Each time your book is printed, it is one print run. Amazon KDP identifies each print run with numbers and a barcode on the last page of the book.

TRADITIONAL PRINTING

Commercial offset printing is an industrial printing process in which ink is transferred from a plate, usually made of metal, onto a rubber sheet, which is then rolled onto a large sheet of paper that is fed through a press. Multiple pages of the book are printed on one large sheet, and then each page is cut to size. Most major publishers print their books using offset printing either in the United States or in a foreign country, like China. **Amazon KDP does not print using offset printers.**

Offset printing requires more cash upfront, somewhere to store the books, and in the case of printing overseas, the books could take as long as 4 to 6 weeks for the author to receive. For large quantities, offset books can be cheaper to print. People who are considering printing 2,000 or more books should consider offset printing, or using a local printer who specializes in printing books digitally if they can get the books for a lower price than they would pay using Amazon KDP. It's best not to commit to printing such a large quantity unless you have a paying customer committed to buying them.

The TRIM SIZE

The **trim size** of a book is the final size of a printed page after excess edges have been cut off. What size do you want your book to be? Would you like it to be similar to one in your library at home or at school? Measure the books you enjoy. Commercial printing companies offer standard book sizes, whether you self-publish or not. Some printers don't just limit the size and orientation of the book; whether the book is wide and short or tall and thin. It's always best to decide on your book's size and orientation before you spend time illustrating it and laying it out.

KDP.amazon.com offers the following trim sizes:

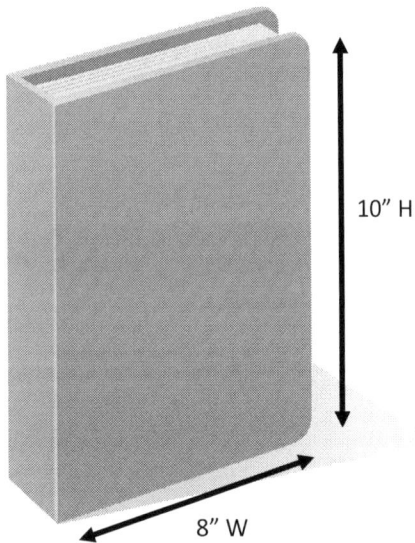

5" W x 8" H
5.06" W x 7.81" H
5.25" W x 8" H
5.5" W x 8.5" H
6" W x 9" H
6.14" W x 9.21"
6.69" W x 9.61" H
7" W x 10" H
7.44" W x 9.69" H
7.5" W x 9.25" H
8" W x 10" H
8.25" W x 6" H
8.25" W x 8.25" H
8.5" W x 8.5" H
8.5" W x 11" H
8.27" W x 11.69" H

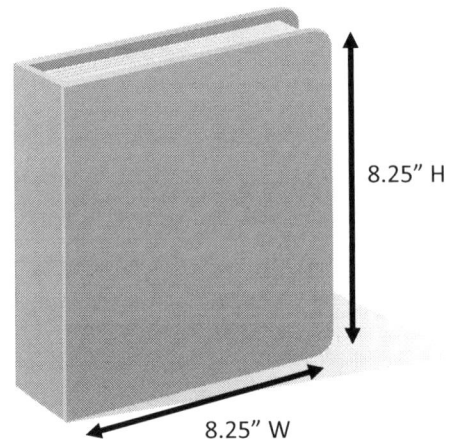

10" H

8" W

8.25" H

8.25" W

Please note that **KDP does not print books with landscape** (wide and short) **orientation,** only orientations that are portrait (tall and thin), or square (even on all sides).

The TRIM SIZE

Authors and illustrators don't want to have images or words cut off when your book goes to the printer, so it's important to know where the printer will trim the pages.

If you are using a template, then there will be crop marks that show you where the paper will be cut. But if you are self-publishing and sizing the book from scratch, know that you will lose .125 inches (⅛ inch) of margin to trimming around each page, so set the margins at .125 inches all around.

To be safe, keep your text and images at least .25 inches (¼ inch) or more from the edge, which combines .125 (⅛ inch) for the trimming and another .125 (⅛ inch) for the safe area. You need to keep all essential illustration within the **safe area**. This way, you won't lose artwork or text when the book is trimmed.

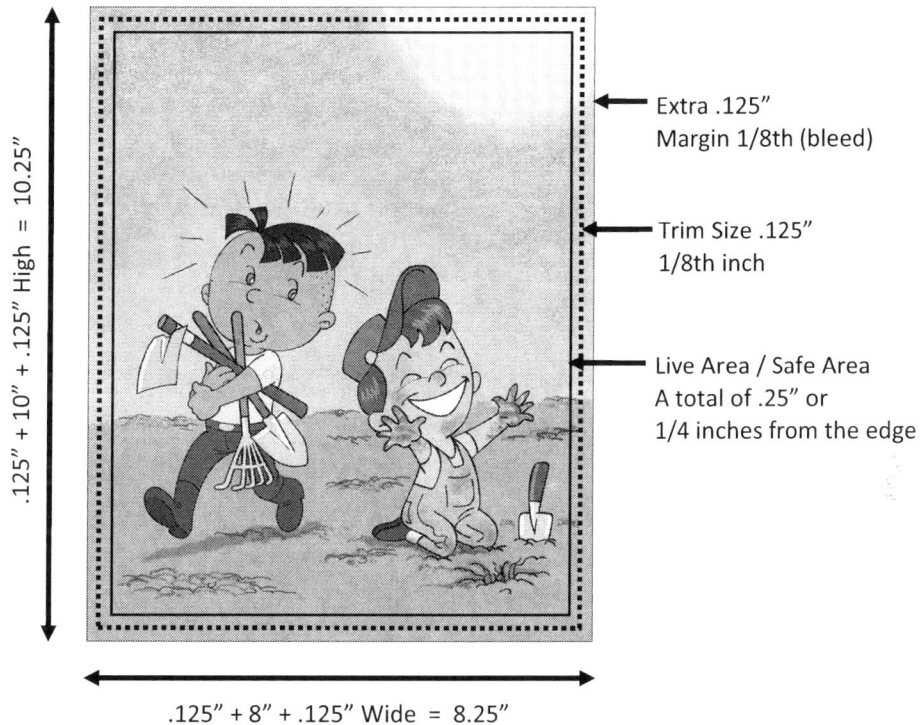

Extra .125"
Margin 1/8th (bleed)

Trim Size .125"
1/8th inch

Live Area / Safe Area
A total of .25" or
1/4 inches from the edge

.125" + 10" + .125" High = 10.25"

.125" + 8" + .125" Wide = 8.25"

Unimportant artwork, like the sky and dirt above, can sit in the margin, just know it will most likely be cut off. Using page layout software makes laying out the book easy to measure from page to page, but you can also set page sizes in a program like Microsoft Publisher or Adobe Photoshop. The margins should be set to .25 inches minimum for every page. Above is an example of an 8" W x 10" H self-published page.

The ARTWORK

The **artwork** is the pictures and illustrations in the book. Whether the artwork is competed digitally or scanned from an original, images and illustration have to be a hi-resolution of 300 dpi (dots per inch) or higher. If you publish your book with low-resolution artwork, the images will come out blurry and pixelated, even if it looks good on your computer. Some self-publishing companies will warn you that your artwork isn't the right resolution in the review process. KDP doesn't always catch this problem.

300 dpi cupcake

low-resolution cupcake

Original artwork should be in CMYK colors, which is standard in the printing industry, but KDP also accepts RGB colors. CMYK is a color model for combining primary pigments. The C stands for cyan (aqua), M stands for magenta (pink), Y for yellow, and K for Key. Set your design program to work in CMYK or RGB before you begin adding color to your illustration. Computers use RGB (Red, Green, Blue) color values, so what you see on your computer monitor may not be what you end up seeing in CMYK print. When using CMYK there are fewer color possibilities than with RGB, so, unfortunately, you can't reproduce many of the vibrant RGB colors with CMYK.

C = Cyan
M = Magenta
Y = Yellow
K = Black

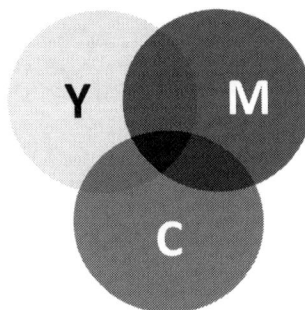

The ARTWORK

Some self-publishing printers, like KDP, will print in CMYK or RGB colors. RGB stands for "Red, Green, Blue." It refers to the three hues of light, that can mix together to form any color. It is safer not to lock yourself into one printing company that only uses CMYK or RGB.

R = Red
G = Green
B = Blue

LAYERING & FLATTENING

When illustrating in design programs, artists place one layer over another. They might draw a shirt on a piece of paper, which would be the first layer, then draw a cat and lay it onto the shirt. The cat would be the 2nd layer. The two combined would make a composition: a shirt with a cat on it. Before uploading any artwork, images should be flattened or combined into one layer. If you are scanning original artwork that you painted or drew yourself, you won't have to worry about layering until you place in your text. A text box adds another layer to your work and might also need to be flattened, or combined. If you don't flatten your images or text boxes, your work could look like it has lines around it. If you don't know what you're doing, saving your pages as commercial press PDFs will usually flatten the work.

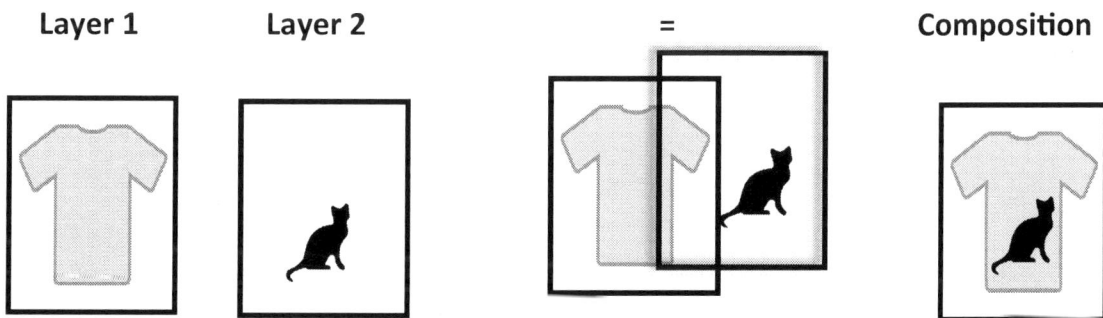

Layer 1	Layer 2	=	Composition

This section is just a quick overview. There is a lot to know when it comes to the artwork. Ask for help, search the internet, take an online tutorial, or take a class to learn more. In the end, it is up to you to request a printed proof of your book to make sure the images are flattened, in focus, and color correct.

Choosing a FONT

A **font** is the STYLE of text printed in a book.

A selection of fonts comes free in whatever writing or design program you use. If you want a specific font, and you can't find it for free, you can buy one that is compatible with your writing or design program from an online designer. If you plan to sell your book, you might have to purchase the commercial rights to use the font you like. Some are free for commercial use, and others are not.

Fonts for children's books should be fun, clean, friendly, simple designs that are easy to read. Look at fonts in popular children's books, and test the font you choose on your friends to see what they think about it.

Here are a few examples of font styles that work for children's books.

Comic Sans	The quick brown fox jumps over the lazy dog.
Century Gothic Pro Reg	The quick brown fox jumps over the lazy dog.
Geo Sans Light	The quick brown fox jumps over the lazy dog.
MV Boli	The quick brown fox jumps over the lazy dog.

Unless there is a very good reason to do so, limit your use to one or two font styles at most. Combining multiple fonts and typefaces distracts from the story and makes the book look messy. Read the two versions of Sam's story below and see how they make you feel.

Sam **THOUGHT** he used TOO **MANY** fonts in **HIS** *REPORT*. They were cool, but now **HIS** **PAPER** looked messy and **cluttered.**

YIKES!

Sam thought he used too many fonts in his report. They were cool, but now his paper looked messy and cluttered.

YIKES!

Decorative fonts, pops of color, and artistic styles can be used to express emotion, emphasize a sound, or attract the reader's attention. Be consistent and use the same format throughout your book. If you use a decorative font to highlight an expression like "Yikes!" be sure to draw attention to feelings on the other pages in a similar manner.

Fonts with ALL CAPITAL letters, **BOLD** typeface, *script*, *italic*, fancy, old English, stylized, or BUSY designs are a strain on the eyes. Here are some examples of fonts that are just "too much" and might make readers dizzy. Can you imagine an entire book written with these fonts?

THE QUICK BROWN FOX JUMPS OVER THE LAZY DOG.

The quick brown fox jumps over the lazy dog.

The quick brown fox jumps over the lazy dog.

The quick brown fox jumps over the lazy dog.

The quick brown fox jumps over the lazy dog.

The quick brown fox jumps over the lazy dog.

It is okay to use playful styles, colors, and layouts in your headlines and titles where there are fewer words to read. Again, be consistent. A font you use for a title on one page should be the same font, size, and typeface used for titles on subsequent pages.

Avoid putting too much text on a page. Early readers might find a lot of words to be intimidating, and even adults like to finish the book by bedtime.

Fonts with letters tight and very close together are condensed and can be difficult to read.

This font is condensed.

This font is not condensed.

The Letters A and G

Young children learn to identify, read, and write the lowercase letter **a**

in the infant or single-story style like this... ***a.***

Instead of

"The boy kicked the **ball**,"

the line should read

"The boy kicked the... **ball**."

For picture books, it is best to use a font with an

infant (single-story) ***a***, since preschoolers and

school-age children are still learning the letters of

the alphabet. Save the two-story **a** for

experienced readers.

Another letter that can be confusing to young

children is the two-story letter **g**

because no one really learns to write the

lowercase **g** like this... **g**.

Instead of

"The girl balanced the **egg**,"

the line should read

"The girl balanced the... **egg**."

Choosing a TYPEFACE

Typeface refers to a family of fonts of a particular design.

Here are examples of typeface in the <u>Comic Sans</u> family of fonts. Pick a typeface and stick with it throughout the book. REGULAR works very well in most cases.

Comic Sans (regular)	The quick brown fox jumps over the lazy dog.
Comic Sans NARROW	The quick brown fox jumps over the lazy dog.
Comic Sans Italic	*The quick brown fox jumps over the lazy dog.*
Comic Sans BOLD Italic	***The quick brown fox jumps over the lazy dog.***
Comic Sans BOLD	**The quick brown fox jumps over the lazy dog.**

Here are examples of the typeface in the <u>Century Gothic</u> family of fonts.

Century Gothic (regular)	The quick brown fox jumps over the lazy dog.
Century Gothic Condensed	The quick brown fox jumps over the lazy dog.
Century Gothic Italic	*The quick brown fox jumps over the lazy dog.*
Century Gothic Italic BOLD	***The quick brown fox jumps over the lazy dog.***
Century Gothic BOLD	**The quick brown fox jumps over the lazy dog.**

Pick a TEXT COLOR

Black is the most common color text on the white pages of children's books, but if you have a black background, then black text obviously won't work. No one will see black on black, so instead use a bright color for the text like white, tan, or yellow. Pick a color that will stand out from the background on each page, making it easier to read.

The Text SIZE

We read from left to right, following the words, jumping our eyes from the end of one line to the beginning of the next line. To make this process easier on new readers, set the text size larger than what you see in books for adults. A good size is 14 to 24 points, depending on the font you choose and the age of the reader. Some fonts are designed to be oversized and will look huge without your changing the size.

Leading is the spacing between lines. Provide very generous spacing. Most publishers recommend four to six points of space between lines. The bigger the font, the more space there will naturally be between the lines. Many large fonts will naturally increase the space between lines. Four points of space separate each sentence below.

<u>FONT: Century Gothic Pro Reg</u>

(14 pt.)   The quick brown fox jumps over the lazy dog.

(16 pt.)   The quick brown fox jumps over the lazy dog.

(20pt.)   The quick brown fox jumps over the lazy dog.

(24 pt.) The quick brown fox jumps over the lazy dog.

The TEXT Placement

Text placement refers to where and how the text is placed on the page.

When speaking, we take natural pauses and breaths to express emotion and give listeners a chance to process what we say. Keep line lengths short. Think about natural pauses in speech when placing text in your book. Read the passage below and take a breath at the end of each line. See how the pauses sound and feel.

Once upon a time, there
was a beautiful princess with long flowing
hair. She had a pet green
dragon who breathed fire and let her ride his tail.

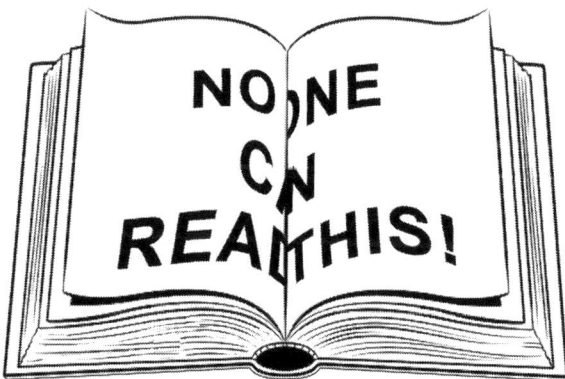

The sentences below flow very smoothly because they pause where we naturally take breaths when we talk. The story sounds more dramatic, and the reader is waiting to see what comes next.

Once upon a time,
there was a beautiful princess
with long flowing hair.
She had a pet green dragon
who breathed fire and let her ride his tail.

NO ONE
CN
REA THIS!

Keep text away from the center margins and out of the gutter. When the book is bound, words can get cut off.

The two most common arrangements for text placement is to have the text on the left side of a two-page spread with the picture on the right or to have the picture on the top and the text on the bottom.

The TITLE and DESCRIPTION

The **title** is a name or phrase that identifies or describes a book. It has to appear on the cover. The title should be short, intriguing, thought-provoking, and to the point. Brainstorm titles by writing down themes, keywords, idioms, catchphrases, rhyming words, and every word or expression that would help readers predict the subject of your book. Arrange these in different combinations to see if anything pops out at you. Try summarizing your work in one sentence, then reducing that sentence down to a phrase. Titles don't have to read like a perfect sentence. A misleading, unclear, or vague title is a missed opportunity to capture a buyer's attention.

- Aim the title toward your audience.
- Keep your title short, simple, and too the point.
- Study titles in your genre and other titles that have caught your attention.
- The title should be written in the primary language of your book.
- Google the topic of your story and see what pops up for inspiration.
- Test your title on friends and family.

The **description** is a short statement or paragraph that explains the subject or topic of a book. After the title and cover, it is the most important part of marketing your book. Carefully select words that express the meaning of your story, and keep revising the description as you think of ways to improve it further.

- Hook the audience with the first sentence so that they will continue reading.
- Write a compelling answer to the question, "Why should someone read this book?"
- Summarize the story without giving away its secrets.
- Stay on point. Avoid overwhelming the reader with useless details.
- Write descriptions that capture the essence of the genre. If you have written a mystery, then make the description mysterious.
- Read descriptions of other books for inspiration.

If you are writing a nonfiction book to educate, then include benefits of reading the book and be specific about what the reader will learn.

The TITLE PAGE and COPYRIGHT PAGE

The **title page** is the first interior page of the book. It announces the title, subtitle, author, illustrator, and publisher of the book. Illustrations are also common on title pages. They can mirror the artwork on the cover or be more decorative as you see here.

COVER

Fruits & Veggies
Making Faces
Written by
Angela Russ-Ayon
Illustrated by
Matt Mew

TITLE PAGE

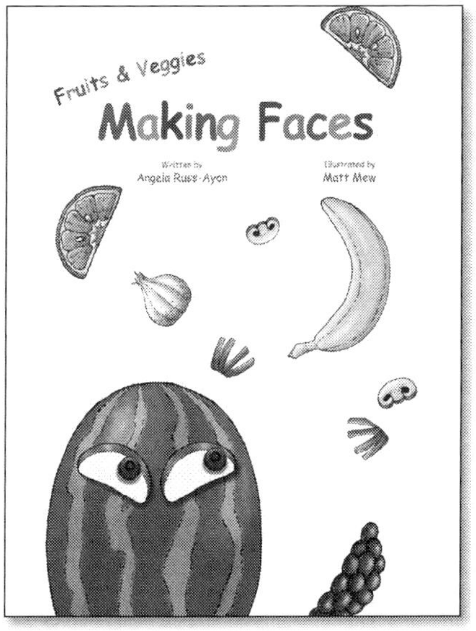

Fruits & Veggies
Making Faces
Written by
Angela Russ-Ayon
Illustrated by
Matt Mew

The **copyright page** is where you print important information about the book. It is usually found on the back side (verso) of the title page at the beginning of the book. This page tells the reader who owns the original work of authorship. As soon as you create your original work, you automatically have a copyright, which prevents others from copying, publishing, or performing your work without your permission. No part of the story goes on the title or copyright pages.

It's important to know that you may not own the copyright if you wrote the book as an employee of a company, or someone paid you to write the book.

You don't have to print all of the information listed below on the Copyright Page, but this information is pretty much standard for every book:

- ☐ The copyright notice - owner of the copyright.
- ☐ The year the book was published.
- ☐ The reservation of rights. Example: *All rights reserved.*
- ☐ The publisher's logo, name, and address or website.
- ☐ The ISBN (International Standard Book Number).

Open a published book for any age and see what is printed on the Copyright Page.

Additional information that can be printed on the copyright page:

- Where the book was printed (City, State, Country).

- The **Library of Congress Number** or **Pre-assigned Control Number (PCN)** is a unique number assigned to a book. Librarians use it to find your book in the national databases. You can print your book without it and add it later. It usually only takes one or two days to be assigned. Here is the link to more information.

  https://www.loc.gov/publish/pcn/

- **Cataloging-in-Publication Data (CIP).** The purpose of the CIP data is to make it easier for libraries to purchase and circulate the book. Without CIP data, librarians have to do the work themselves to determine what the book is about and assign classification numbers. The CIP block is not required for publishing.

CIP data is specific to the book it catalogs; you cannot reuse the CIP data block you used on other titles or editions of your book. Nor can you use someone else's CIP data. You get the CIP block either from the Library of Congress or from another source for a fee - usually before the book is published.

If you publish through Amazon KDP, you can always add details to your copyright page later.

Here is additional information that can be printed on the copyright page:

- The edition of the book (1st edition, 2nd edition, etc.).
- Numbers that identify the print run help you remember exactly when your book was printed. If there is a problem with the printing, you can identify the entire batch of defective books.
- Contact information for the author and illustrator.
- Short biographies of the author and illustrator.
- A list of other books the author has published. This is a chance to promote other books you have written. If someone likes your book, they might look for others you have published.
- Some publishers use the copyright page to give credit to special contributors to the book like designers, proofreaders, and copyeditors.

When you create your copyright page, pick the information that seems most suitable and relevant to your book.

If you liked that, here's what else I've written!

About the COPYRIGHT NOTICE and RESERVATION RIGHTS

You'll want to declare to readers that you own the rights to your work or story with a copyright notice. The job of the copyright notice is to tell the reader that you are the person who wrote the words or story and you are the owner of the copyright. The notice can be written one of these three ways.

Copyright © Anthony Hall, 2019. All Rights Reserved.
Copyright © 2019 Anthony Hall. All Rights Reserved.
Copyright © 2019 by Anthony Hall. All Rights Reserved.

It consists of four components:

1. "Copyright": Your book may be published in other countries, so you want to spell out the word "copyright" before the symbol, so there is no confusion.
2. ©: This is the universal symbol for copyright in the United States and most countries.
3. Copyright owner's name: This would be the creator's name, but it is okay to use a pen name or pseudonym.
4. Year of publication: This is the year you publish the story, not the year you first created the story or got the idea for it.

Also, registering your copyright with the U.S. Copyright office gives you specific legal advantages and protects you against copycats. Here is the link for more information:

https://www.copyright.gov

Here is a sample of a copyright page in a book. The copyright notice and ISBN have to appear on the copyright page, no matter what.

Other titles by this author:
We Eat Food That's Fresh, with Companion CD
Comemos Comida Fresca, English & Spanish
Fruits & Veggies Making Faces
We Love the Company, A Book About Table Manners, with Companion CD
When You Find Colors and Shapes
Cuando Encuentres los Colores y las Formas, English & Spanish

Author: Angela Russ-Ayon
Illustrator: José Gascón H.

1st edition

For information about permission to reproduce selections of this book, contact:

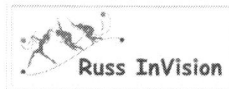

Russ InVision Company
3219 Conquista Ave., Long Beach, CA 90808
E-mail: info@abridgeclub.com
www.abridgeclub.com

ISBN: 978-0-9987090-3-1

Library of Congress Control Number: 2018911434

Copyright © 2018 Russ InVision Company. All rights reserved.

No part of this publication may be reproduced in any form or by any means,
without prior written permission from Russ InVision Company.

Author: Angela Russ-Ayon, Illustrator: José Gascón H
Publisher: Russ InVision Company, Long Beach, CA 90808, www.abridgeclub.com
ISBN 13: ISBN 978-0-9987090-3-1 English pbk.
Names: Russ-Ayon, Angela, author | José Gascón H, illustrator.
Title: Fruits and veggies in row by row: children in the garden
/ written by Angela Russ-Ayon; illustrated by José Gascón H.
Summary: A diverse group of children works together to grow fruits
and vegetables in the garden from seed to sprout to harvest.
Description: Long Beach, CA: Russ InVision Company, 2018.
Identifiers: ISBN 978-0-9987090-3-1 | LCCN 2018911434
Subjects: LCSH Nutrition—Juvenile literature. | Food—Juvenile literature |
Fruit—Juvenile literature | Vegetables—Juvenile literature. |
Health—Juvenile literature. | BISAC JUVENILE FICTION / GARDENING |
JUVENILE FICTION / Health & Daily Living / General
Classification: LCC PZ7.R8999 We 2017 | DDC [E]—dc23

International Standard Book Number (ISBN)

The **International Standard Book Number** (ISBN) is a unique number assigned to each edition of a printed book. If you want your printed book on shelves in either bookstores or libraries, you'll need an ISBN. The ISBN is what retail stores and libraries use to keep track of books.

If you see a book you like, and you want to buy a copy for yourself, all you need is the ISBN to find the same book in a bookstore or online because one ISBN matches only one published book. You cannot use the same ISBN on different books or different versions of books. **KDP will provide you with a free ISBN to publish your paperback.**

An ISBN identifies:

- the specific title, edition, and author
- the country or language of the book
- the publisher of the book
- the format & physical properties (binding, size, number of pages, etc.)

You can find the ISBN along with the barcode on the lower right corner of the back of a printed book, and again on the copyright page. All physical copies have ISBNs assigned.

None of the top **eBook** retailers such as Amazon, Apple, Barnes & Noble, or Kobo require an ISBN, but some authors assign one to every version of their books as a way of keeping track of what they've published. It's interesting to take note that many bestselling Kindle books on Amazon don't have ISBNs assigned.

The ISBN

Every ISBN has 13 digits. Up until January 1, 2007, ISBNs only had ten numbers, so some books have both 10 and 13 digit ISBNs. Here is an example of the ISBN for the 32-page, perfect bound, paperback version of a book entitled *Fruits and Veggies, Row by Row*. Try entering this number in a Google search without the dashes to see what comes up.

ISBN 13: 978-0-9987090-3-1

Once an ISBN is assigned to your paperback and the book is published, you can't change the author's name, book's binding, the size of the book, or the number of pages, but you can publish a new version of the book with a new ISBN. If you have a hardback and a paperback version of a book, you have to have two different ISBNs. If one book has 32 pages, and the other has 100, you have to have two different ISBNs. If two books are two different sizes, you have to have two different ISBNs. If one book is color and the other is black and white, you will need two different ISBNs. If you change the name of the book after it is published, you will need to acquire a new ISBN for the new title. You can change the cover design, words and illustration on the interior pages, the price, and the description of the book, without having to change the ISBN.

You don't have to buy an ISBN for your book when you publish with KDP, but some authors purchase a block of ISBNs because they want their trade or company name to be associated with every book they publish. The United States ISBN Agency is the only agency authorized to assign ISBNs to publishers in the United States, U.S. Virgin Islands, Guam, and Puerto Rico. You can purchase ISBNs in blocks of 10, 100, and 1000. KDP authors are allowed to buy one ISBN or a batch of ISBNs at a discounted rate from Bowker.

Here is the link to more information for purchasing ISBNs:

https://www.isbn.org
(by Bowker)

The BARCODE

ISBN 978-0-9891631-5-6

51699

9 780989 163156

A **barcode** is a series of printed lines of varying width that can be read by an optical scanner. It is different from an ISBN. Lines and bars on a barcode make it easier for retail stores and distributors to identify your book by scanning the bars (or lines) with an electronic tool, instead of typing all 13 numbers of the ISBN. Retail stores use barcodes to keep track of inventory, sell books at the cash register, and avoid human error. If sellers had to type thirteen numbers into the register every time a customer purchased a book, there would definitely be a lot of human error.

The barcode identifies:
- the ISBN number
- the type of money or currency in which the book is being sold
- the price of the book

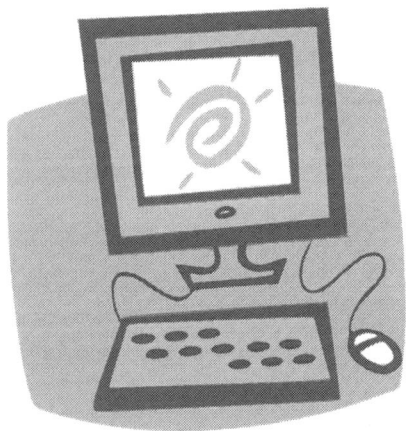

Can you find the $16.99 price in the barcode above?

You don't automatically get a barcode when you buy an ISBN, but whether you buy an ISBN or get one free from KDP, **KDP will generate a barcode for you**. All you have to do is leave space for a 2" by 1.2" white box in the lower right-hand corner of the book's back cover. If you put text or artwork in that space, it will get covered up by the barcode that is placed there.

Although you don't need to with KDP, if you provide your own barcode, there is a box you check to let them know.

Barcodes can have different looks to them, whereas an ISBN for a particular book always remains the same.

REJECTION

Rejection in publishing refers to someone not accepting your work, for whatever reason and not offering to publish your book. It is not personal. **You don't have to worry about Amazon KDP rejecting your self-published book.** They will print almost any book you submit as long as you have followed their guidelines, uploaded the files correctly, and have not stolen someone else's work.

If you choose not to self-publish and decide to submit your manuscript to a traditional publisher who can print your book, your book will either be accepted or rejected. Authors are very familiar with the term "rejection."

Imagine that you send your manuscript to an editor, and the editor doesn't like your book. He or she is a person who has opinions, life experiences, challenges, goals, and ideas that may not align with yours. Rejection is subjective: based on or influenced by personal feelings, tastes, or opinions. If a person had a bad experience in middle school, they might not like stories that center around middle school.

Think of rejection as a garage sale where you are selling your personal treasures. One person will walk right past your prized possession and think it's junk, and another person will stop and say, "I can't believe I found one of these!"

Editors review your manuscript at a traditional publishing house. They may reject your book because of a variety of reasons.

- Your story isn't unique or fresh enough. The editors have other stories just like yours. Your book doesn't have a clever enough hook or theme that will make it stand out from other books in the marketplace.
- Your story is missing something. It could be lacking an apparent conflict, a firm resolution, character development, or any number of things.
- The publisher doesn't handle your type of story. You wrote a mystery, and they publish romances. They publish autobiographies, and you wrote a fairytale.
- Your story isn't written for the publisher's audience. They publish board books for babies, and yours is a picture book for preschoolers.
- Your story just doesn't "wow" them.

If traditional publishers don't want your story, don't give up. Self-publish your book and prove them wrong. You may attract their attention by selling an impressive number of copies. Just remember, you can't please EVERYONE. Once your book is published, there will still be critics who leave feedback and reviews that may not be flattering, or even nice.

POPULAR REJECTED BOOKS!

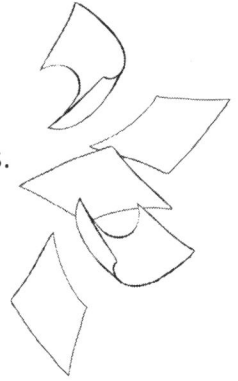

See if you recognize any of these well-known authors and their rejected books.

- **_The Giving Tree,_** by Shel Silverstein
  Shel was told, _"This book will never sell."_ It sold over five million copies.

- **_Harry Potter,_** by J. K. Rowling
  This book was rejected over ten times by the biggest publishing houses. It finally sold after one agent's eight-year-old daughter nagged him into taking on the book. It has made over 10 billion dollars in books, movies, toys, collectibles, and theme park experiences.

- **_Wizard of Oz,_** by L. Frank Baum
  This book was rejected so many times that Frank kept a rejection journal called "A Record of Failure." It is now one of the best known American stories, has been translated into multiple languages, and has been adapted into films and musicals.

- **_The Tale of Peter Rabbit,_** by Beatrix Potter
  This book was rejected so many times that Beatrix decided to self-publish 250 copies. It has since sold 45 million copies and been made into a movie.

- **_A Wrinkle in Time_**, by Madeleine L'Engle
  Twenty-six publishers rejected this book. It won a 1963 Newberry Medal, became an international best-seller, has sold over 8 million copies, and was made into a movie twice.

- **_The One in the Middle Is the Green Kangaroo,_** by Judy Blume
  Judy's first book was rejected for two years. She tells writers, "Each time I sent a story or book off to a publisher, I would sit down and begin something new. Don't let anyone discourage you."

- **Books by Dr. Seuss**
  Dr. Seuss was told that his books were "too different from other juveniles on the market to warrant its selling." He has 300 million in sales and is the 9th best-selling fiction author of all time.

UPLOADING Your BOOK to KDP

To upload your book, you have to use a computer and open an account with Amazon KDP. Children may need their parents to help enter some of the required information.

https://kdp.amazon.com

You need to have the following:

- a hi-resolution PDF spread of your book (cover and back).
- a hi-resolution PDF of your interior pages, which includes the title page and the copyright page.
- an accurate, attention-grabbing description of your book.
- keywords that describe and help buyers find your book.
- an idea of the category for your book. KDP provides categories from which to choose.
- an idea of what the price of your book will be. Browse through Amazon.com for similar books to get an idea of how to price yours.

The KDP system will not allow you to publish a book that has glaring errors, like the improperly sized pages, text that falls outside of the margin, or mix-matched titles, and will display ERRORS on the left margin. Keep in mind that the KDP system and reviewers don't catch everything. They have no personal interest in your book. It is up to you to find any problems.

Don't be surprised if you need to upload revised versions of your book's interior and cover files multiple times before you get it right. It's pretty normal. Even after your book is published, you can resubmit your files and make some changes, but when your book goes live on Amazon, anyone can purchase the live version until you make your revisions.

After your book is published, KDP will contact you with a "quality waring" if readers report problems with your book. Put your best work out there, because it should not come to that.

LOG IN to your account on

https://kdp.amazon.com

KDP will step you through all of the questions in this order:

✹ PAPERBACK DETAILS:

1. Begin at the **BOOKSHELF** on the upper left side of the KDP page.
2. Select "+ Paperback" under **CREATE TITLE** and answer the questions as they appear.
3. Choose your paperback's **PRIMARY LANGUAGE**.
4. Enter your book's **TITLE** as it appears on the book's cover.
5. Enter your book's **SUBTITLE**. It is not required, and if you have one, it does not have to appear on the cover of the book. The subtitle is used as an extension of the title to explain, describe, or clarify the title or book's topic. On KDP, the subtitle will appear as a continuation of the title, separated by a colon (:).
6. Enter your book's **SERIES** information. Here is an example from the *Lord of the Rings* series of books: Series name: "The Fellowship of the Ring." Series number: 1
7. Enter the **VERSION** number, if this is one of multiple versions of your book.
8. Enter the full **AUTHOR's NAME**.
9. Add any **CONTRIBUTORS** one at a time. (The illustrator or editor)
10. Enter your book's **DESCRIPTION**. KDP limits the number of characters to 4000.
11. Enter up to eight **KEYWORDS** and popular search phrases.
12. Choose up to two browsing **CATEGORIES**. (Fiction, nonfiction, and sub-categories)
13. Enter whether there is **ADULT CONTENT** in your book. Yes or no? There shouldn't be since you have written a children's picture book.
14. **SAVE** your entries.

❂ PAPERBACK CONTENT:

15. Select whether you want KDP to assign an **ISBN**, or enter one you purchased. Enter the company or trade name to which the purchased ISBN is linked.

16. Enter the **PUBLICATION DATE** for our book. If you don't enter a date, KDP will use the date your book goes live on Amazon.com.

17. Select your **PRINT OPTIONS**.
    ⇒ Black and white with cream interior pages.
    ⇒ Black and white with white interior pages.
    ⇒ Color interior pages with white paper. (This is most common.)

18. Select which **TRIM SIZE** you would like your book to be. What are the dimensions (width and height) of your book. You will have set the dimensions of your book in the design program you used.

19. Indicate whether there is a **BLEED** (artwork all the way to the edge of the pages), or no bleed.

20. Select a **FINISH** for the cover. Matte or glossy? (Glossy is most common.)

21. Upload your **MANUSCRIPT** as one formatted PDF file. You can also upload a DOC (.doc), DOCX (.docx), HTML (.html), or RTF (.rtf).

22. Upload the spread of the **COVER AND BACK** as one PDF. Design your own cover or create a cover using KDP's Cover Creator tool. KDP has commercial-free stock images you can use. Check the box if you are providing your own **BARCODE**.

23. Preview your cover and interior pages to check for any formatting issues by clicking on **LAUNCH PREVIEWER**. This may take a few minutes. The preview allows you to flip through your book from cover to back as if you were holding it in your hands.

    Now is the time to check your book page-by-page for mistakes in formatting. Putting a book together is a complicated process with many steps. **ERRORS** will appear on the left bar with the pages that have issues. Click on each page number and KDP will display what is wrong. There is a lot to juggle so take your time. See page 89 for help on proofreading.

24. **SAVE** and continue.

❋ PAPERBACK RIGHTS and PRICING:

25. Select the **TERRITORIES** for which you hold distribution rights. Worldwide or select countries? If this is your original work, you hold worldwide rights.

26. The primary marketplace for the United States is Amazon.com. The **LIST PRICE** is the retail price you want the book to sell for on Amazon.com. It is the price the public will see on Amazon's detail page. KDP displays the minimum and maximum retail price it will allow. It will also display your **PRINTING COST** and the **ROYALTY** they will pay per region under "other marketplaces."

27. Select **EXPANDED DISTRIBUTION** if you want to reach more readers by distributing your paperback through bookstores, online retailers, libraries, and academic institutions. You don't have to select this option. You can select it later.

28. Click here to order and pay for one to five **PROOF COPIES** of your book, which you can purchase through your Amazon shopping cart. The proofs will all come with a gray **watermark** across the middle of the cover that says "Not for Resale." Traditional publishing houses use the same type of watermark. It is standard in the industry. Proofs are for reviewing your work and sending your book to professional reviewers who are not supposed to sell your book.

At this point, you can save your book as a **DRAFT** and continue to make changes now or later, or **PUBLISH YOUR PAPERBACK BOOK**.

It can take up to 72 hours for your book to be available for purchase on Amazon. Until then, the book's status will be "In Review" on your **BOOKSHELF**.

You will receive an email from Amazon KDP when your book is published that says, **"Congratulations, the paperback edition of your book is live in the Amazon Store!"**

It's time to create your author page, make an audiobook, work on your e-book, and begin marketing your picture book if you haven't started already.

PROOFREADING Your BOOK

Proofreading is finding and correcting mistakes in a story before the final copies are printed. Here are some problems to watch out for when you launch the previewer and after you receive a physical proof of your book:

◊ Make sure you spelled your title correctly on the book and the KDP form.

◊ Confirm that you spelled your name correctly on the cover and the KDP form.

◊ Verify that you spelled your illustrator's or any contributor's names correctly on the cover, and the KDP form.

◊ Double-check the ISBN and other information on the copyright page.

◊ Confirm that the ISBN on the barcode matches the one on the copyright page.

◊ Make sure the barcode on the back doesn't cover anything important.

◊ Check the layout for text and images that are too close to the edge, over the margin, or in the gutter.

◊ Watch for low-resolution images that might be blurry and fuzzy, or stretched and distorted.

◊ See if the images are color correct.

◊ Check if your images are formatted the same: with or without borders, shadows, custom frames, etc.

◊ Make sure all lists are in numerical or alphabetical order.

◊ Check to see that your table of contents or glossary page numbers are correct.

◊ If you referred to something in your book, such as a diagram or chart, make sure the reference numbers or letters match up with the text.

◊ See if the text printed on all of the pages and that no words are missing.

◊ Confirm that the text is all in the same font, style, and size.

◊ Check for unusual and uneven line spacing.

◊ Double check grammar, spelling, and punctuation.

◊ Do all of the paragraphs begin the same, with or without indentions or fancy letters? Do they all start in the same positions?

◊ Look for missing pages.

◊ Check that the pages are in order.

◊ Pages don't need to be numbered, but if they are, are they numbered correctly?

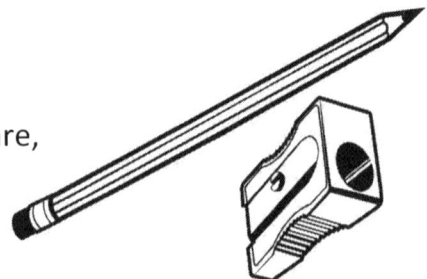

PROMOTING Your BOOK

If no one knows about your book, you probably won't sell very many. You have to promote and actively support it in the marketplace. Write an excellent description and type the right keywords on KDP's detail page to help people find your book. **Keywords** are words and short phrases that define the subject of your book. Thousands of people type keywords into search engines like Google.com to find books every day. For example, a mother might search using the keyword phrase "book about going to the doctor" on Amazon.com or Google to find a book for her child. Look for other creative ways to promote and **publicize** your book to make it widely known. Here are a few suggestions, some of which you can do before you publish.

- Build a website.
- Solicit schools for author visits.
- Offer to read your book at bookstores, libraries, and special events.
- Attend conferences and book fairs.
- Write articles and blogs about the subject of your book.
- Inform local newspapers, online bloggers, radio stations, and talk show host about your book.
- Send mailings and e-mailers to potential customers.
- Establish a social media presence with posts, images, video, and quotes.
- Start an online discussion about the subject of your book.
- Connect your story to trending topics.
- Submit your book for book reviews and literary awards.
- Spend the money for small promotional items like bookmarks, postcards, or coloring pages.
- Invite friends and family over for a reading.
- Send free copies to people who are in a position to buy the book.

STORYBOARD

Use this template to plan out your book by drawing rough sketches and writing brief descriptions. Enter page numbers in the circles. Copy these pages as needed.

STORYBOARD

STORYBOARD

STORYBOARD

STORYBOARD

STORYBOARD

STORYBOARD

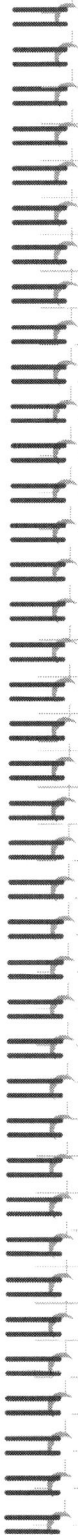

NOTES

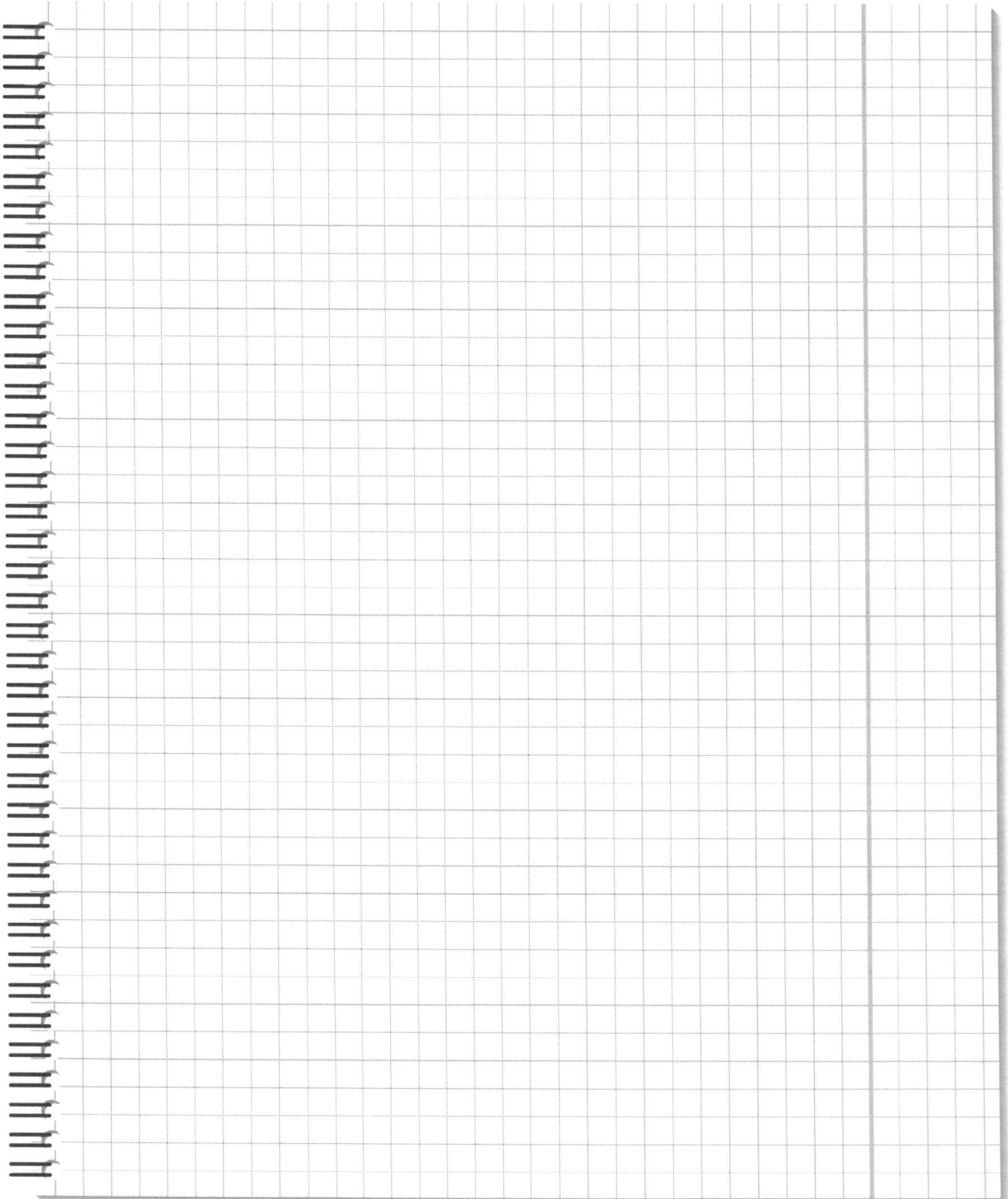

NOTES

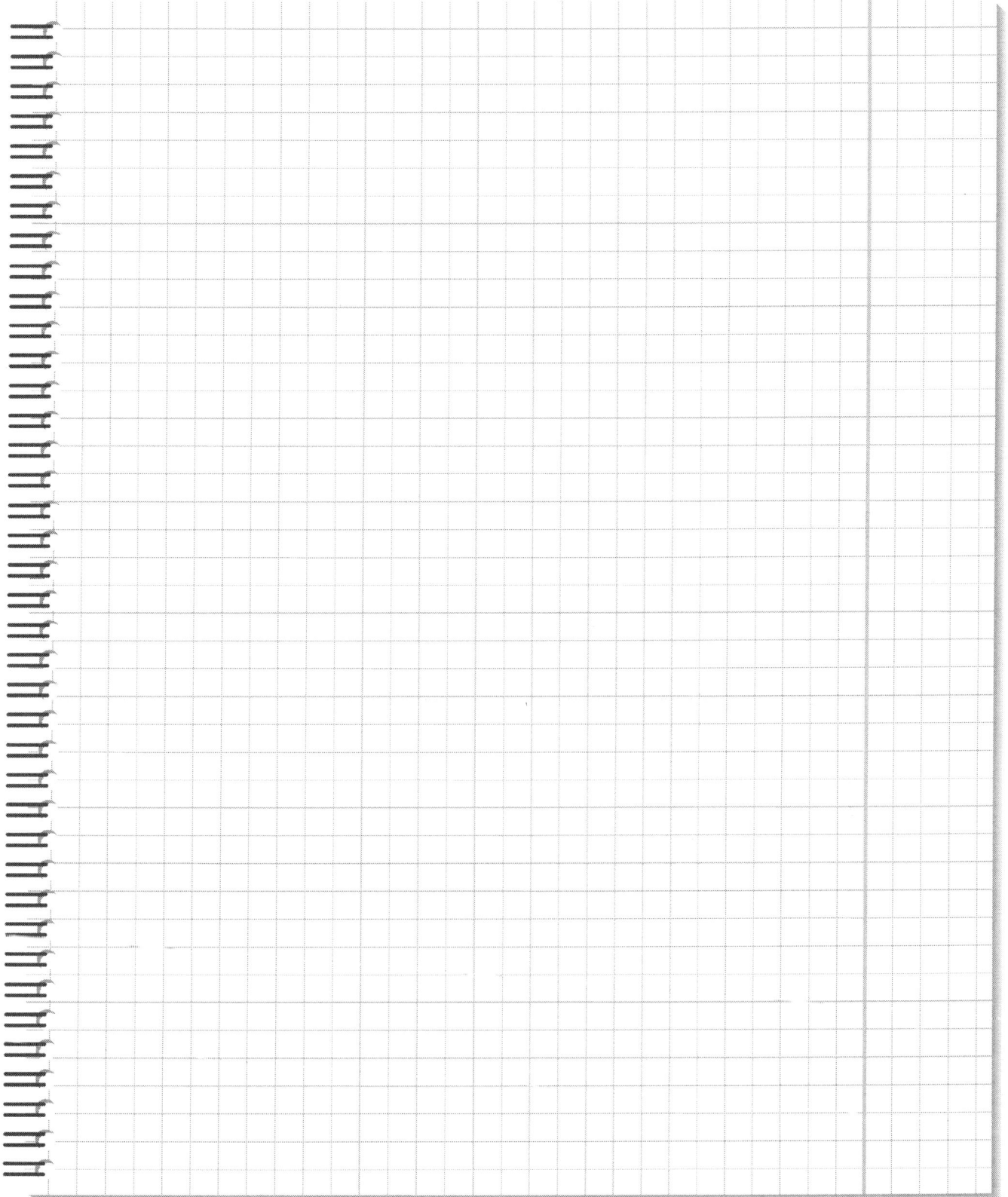

NOTES

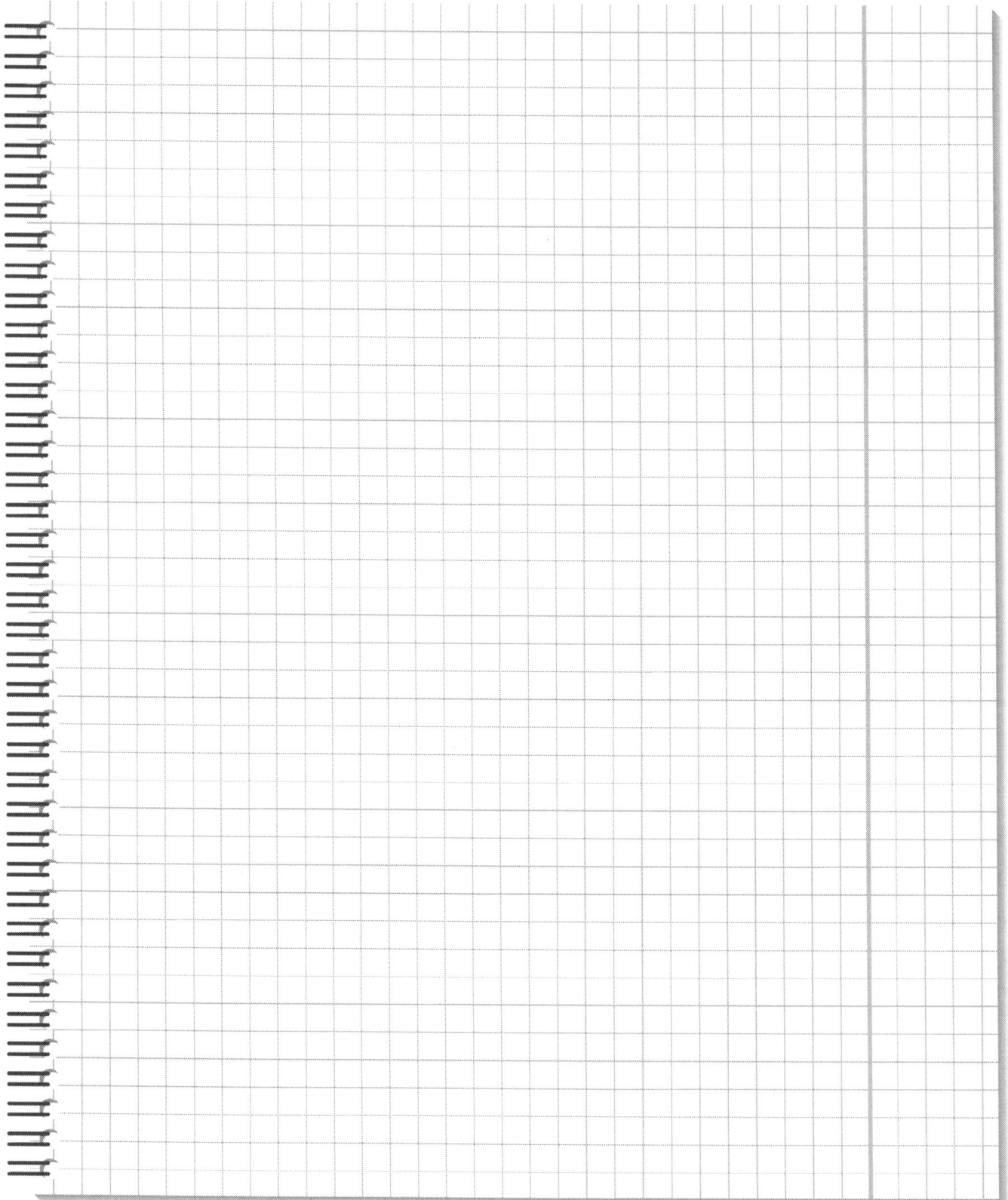

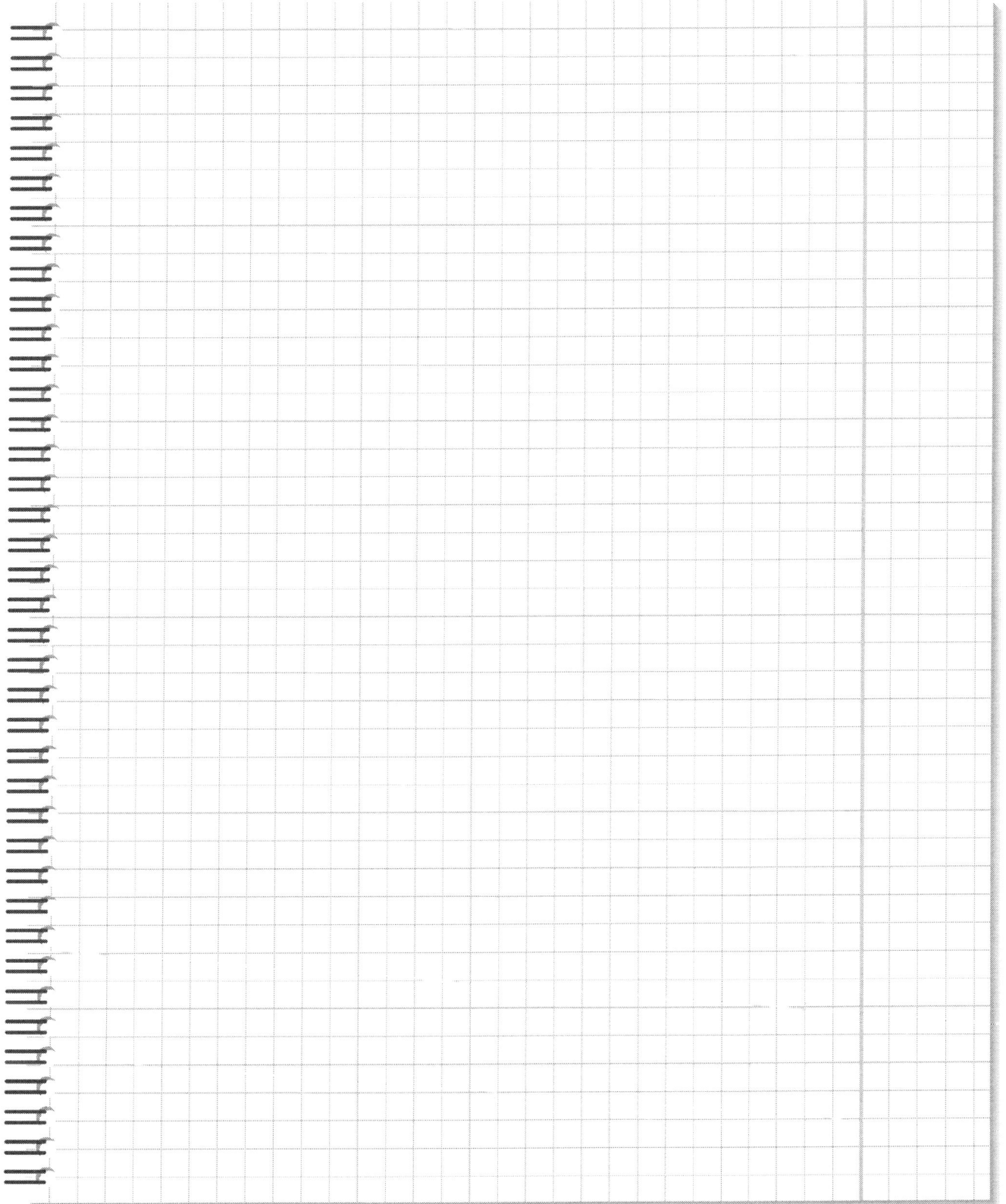

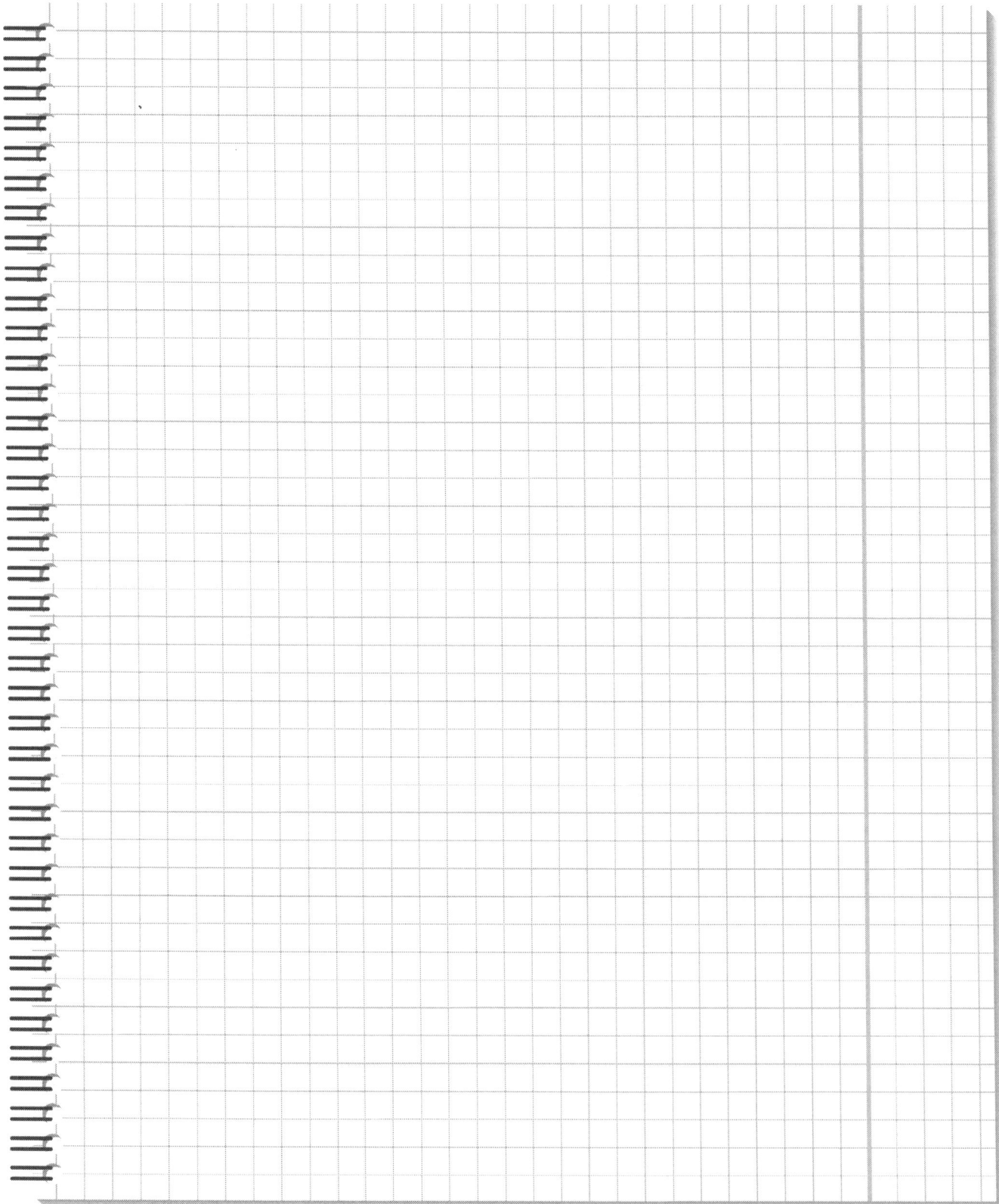

NOTES

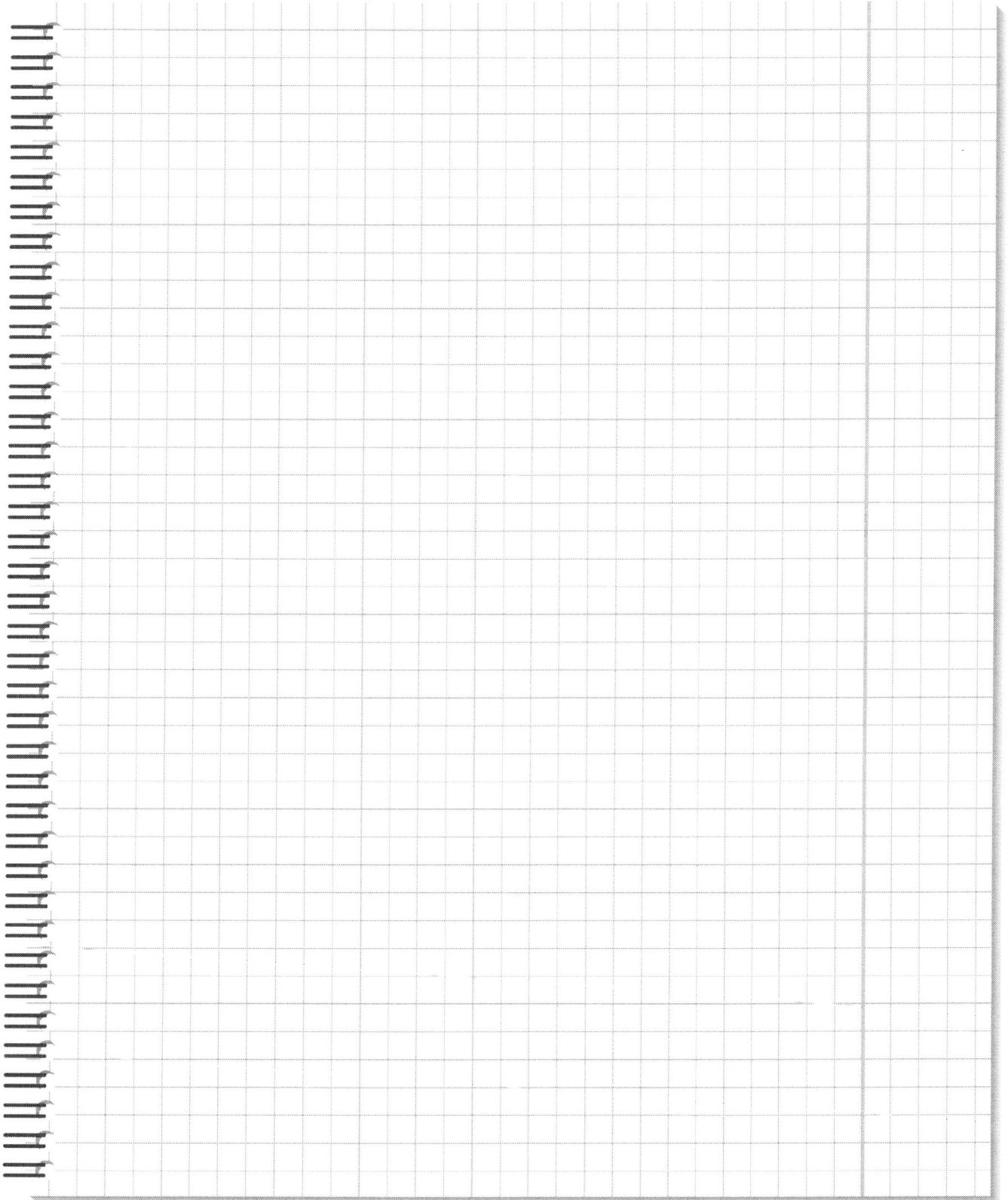

NOTES

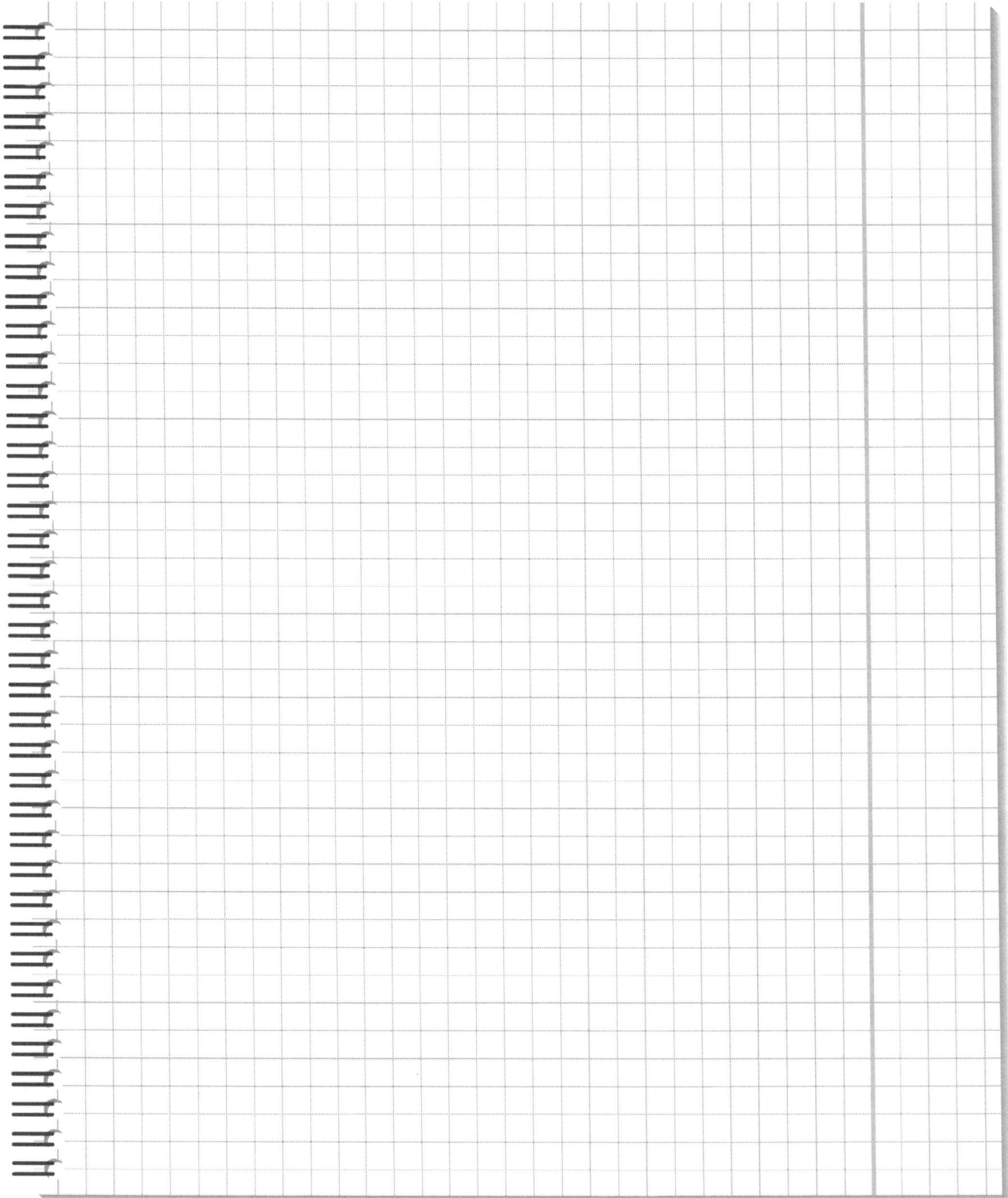

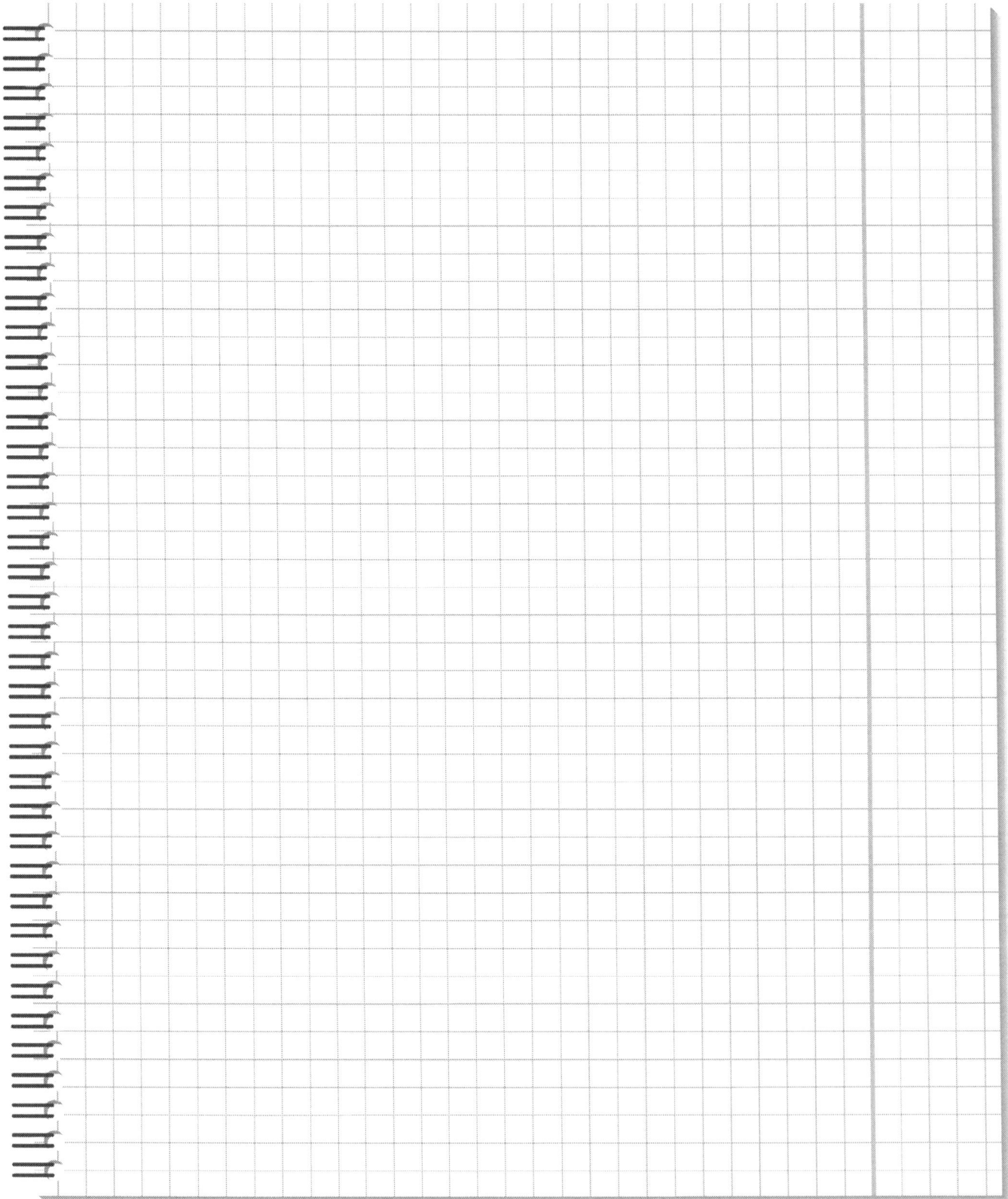

NOTES

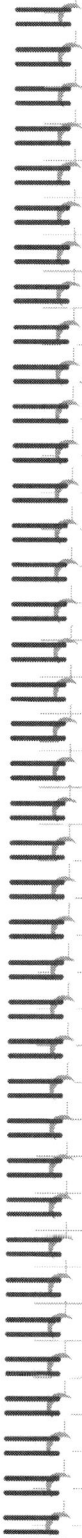

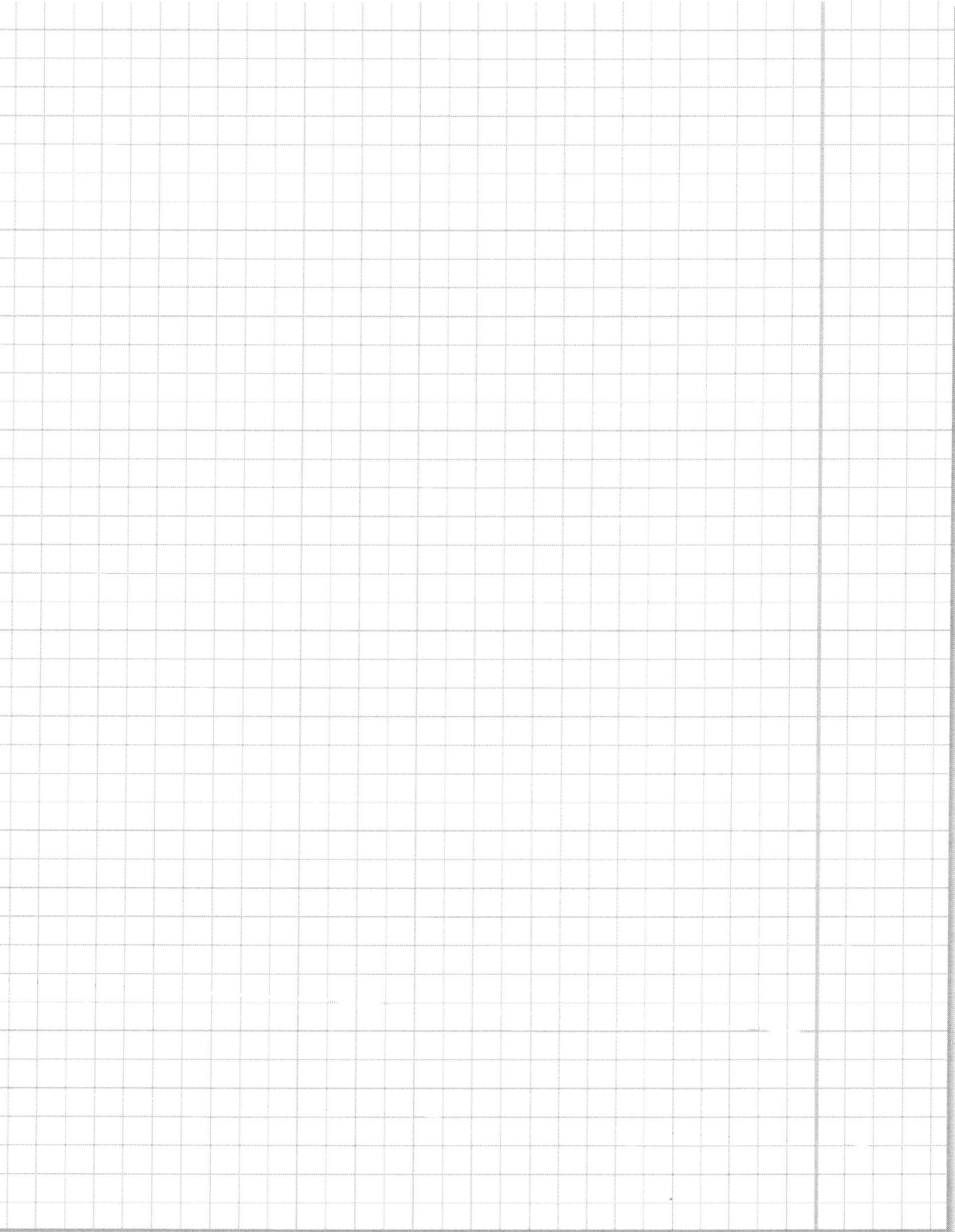

GLOSSARY

Adhesive casebound	Books bound with adhesive and encased in a hard cover. (pg. 57)
Advance	The money paid to the author and illustrator by a traditional publishing house at the beginning of the publishing process, sometimes in installments. (pg. 14)
Amazon KDP	A fast, free and full-service for authors to self-publish their books in digital format to a global audience (pg. 8)
Artwork	The pictures and illustrations in a book.
Back (of book)	The thick protective outer part you see when you flip over a book. (pg. 46)
Barcode	A series of printed lines of varying width that can be read by an optical scanner. (pg. 82)
Binding	The material that holds the pages of a book together, especially the cover. (pg. 56)
Blank pages	The unused pages of a book. (pg. 52)
Bleed	Printing that goes beyond the edge of where the pages are trimmed. (pg. 55)
Board books	A book for very small children or babies, with the pages pasted to heavy cardboard, making them very thick. (pg. 57)
Border	A narrow strip of color or ornamental design along an edge of a page, text box, or picture. (pg. 55)
Cataloging-in-Publication Data (CIP)	A bibliographic record prepared by the Library of Congress for a book that has not yet been published. (pg. 76)
CMYK	A color model for combining primary pigments. The C stands for cyan (aqua), M stands for magenta (pink), Y for yellow, and K for Key. (pgs. 64, 65)
Coil binding	A method of binding where a single spiraled piece of wire or plastic is wound through holes at the edges of loose-leaf pages.
Color palette	A range of colors. (pg. 42)
Commercial offset printing	An industrial printing process in which ink is transferred from a plate, usually made of metal, onto a rubber sheet, which is then rolled onto a large sheet of paper that is fed through a press. (pg. 61)
Commercial-free	The use of images to make money or in any sort of "for-profit" or promotional endeavor. (pg. 39)
Content	The subject the writing deals with, the story that the writing tells, or the ideas that the writing expresses. (pg. 27)
Conventions	A way in which something is usually done, especially within a particular area or activity. (pg. 27)
Copyeditor	A person who edits a manuscript to find and correct errors in style, punctuation, and grammar. (pg. 34)
Copyright infringement	To use work that is protected by copyright law without permission, such as reproducing, distributing, displaying in public, or performing the protected work - or imitating the work of another person. (pg. 39)
Copyright notice	A notice that identifies who owns the rights to written work, a story, book, etc. (pg. 78)
Copyright page	The second interior page of the book where important information about the book is printed (pg. 75)
Copyright-free	The right to use copyright material or intellectual property without having to pay for it. (pg. 39)
Cover (of book)	The thick protective outer part on the front that displays the title, an image that will attract a buyer, and the name of the author and illustrator. (pg. 46)
Description	A short statement or paragraph that explains the subject or topic of a book. (pg. 74)
Dialog	A conversation between two people. (pg. 23)
Diversity	The inclusion of different types of people. An understanding that each individual is unique. (pg. 20)
E-books	Downloadable books that can be read on devices such as tablets, phones, and computers. (pg. 59)
Edit	To prepare written work to be published or used: make changes, condense, rearrange, correct mistakes, etc. (pg. 38)
Emotion	A state of mind that result from one's circumstances, a mood: happy, sad, mad, embarrassed, depressed, etc. (pg. 32)

Expanded distribution	Access to a larger audience through more online retailers, bookstores, libraries, academic institutions, and distributors within the United States. (pg. 89)
Fiction	Stories created from one's imagination. (pg. 16)
Finish	The surface appearance of a manufactured material or object, i.e., glossy or matte. (pg. 87)
First person POV	Someone is telling the reader his or her story, including thoughts, opinions, emotions, actions, and so on, using "I" or "we." (pg. 35)
Five senses	The faculties of sight, smell, hearing, taste, and touch. (pg. 23)
Flattening	A process that combines all the layers in artwork into a single background layer. (pg. 65)
Font	The style of text printed in a book. (pg. 66)
Front matter	The first section of a book; also sometimes called the prelims or preliminary matter. It can include the title page, copyright page, foreword, a preface, etc. (pg. 49)
Genre	A particular category of book, like science fiction, thriller, horror, comedy, action and adventure, romance, autobiography, and so on. (pg. 12, 18)
Glossary	an alphabetical list of terms or words found in text or relating to a specific subject with explanations; a brief dictionary. (pgs. 52, 112)
Glossy	In relation to the cover of a book, glossy is the shiny surface. (pg. 47)
Google	A search engine on the internet located at Google.com. (pgs. 10, 31, 33, 34, 39, 81)
Grammar	The set of rules that explains how words change their form and combine with other words in a language. (pg. 33)
Gutter (of book)	The inside margins closest to the spine of a book or the blank space between two facing pages in the center of a book. The part that runs down the middle of a spread. (pg. 47)
Hardcover books	Books with hard, durable covers. (pg. 56)
Illustration	A picture, design, or diagram. (pg. 39)
Interior pages	The set of pages or leaves on the inside of a book. (pgs. 47, 48)
International Standard Book Number (ISBN)	A unique number that assigned to every book before publication that identifies the book by recording such details as language, country of origin, and publisher. (pgs. 80, 81)
ISBN	International Standard Book Number (pgs. 80, 81)
KDP	Kindle Direct Publishing, by Amazon. (pg. 8)
Keywords	Keywords are words and short phrases that define the subject of your book. (pg. 92)
Layering	The act of placing one design or part of an illustration over another. (pg. 65)
Layout	The arrangement of text, images, pages, and other objects. (pgs. 50, 51)
Leading	The space between lines of text. (pg. 72)
Leaf (in book)	The page of a book or a sheet of paper in a pile. (pg. 47)
Library of Congress	The largest library in the United States with a classification system for every book in the nation. (pg. 76)
Literary agent	A professional agent who acts on behalf of an author in dealing with publishers and others to promote the author's work. (pg. 15)
Logical order	The facts, information, or research reasonably or sensibly organized in a way that something would happen, or in a way that makes sense. (pg. 27)
Main character	A person or other being who is the major focus of the story, has a major role in the plot, and/or interacts regularly with main characters. (pg. 19)
Manuscript	An original book, document, or piece of music written by hand or typed, that has not been published. (pg. 12)
Matte	In relation to the cover of a book, a surface that is dull and flat with no shine. (pg. 47)
Medium	The material or form used by an artist, composer, or writer, such as pen and ink, watercolor, acrylic paint, pastel chalk, etc. (pg. 40)
Near rhyme	Rhyming in which the words sound the same but do not rhyme perfectly. (pg. 37)
Nonfiction	A story or writing that is based on fact. (pg.27)
Orientation	The physical position or direction of something. i.e. portrait (tall and thin) vs. landscape (long and wide).
Page count	The number of pages in the interior of a book. (pg. 49)
Paper color	The color of paper inside of the book. (pg. 48)

Paper weight	The weight of the paper or thickness of the paper stock used to make a book. (pg. 48)
Paperback books	Books with covers that are printed on cover stock, or heavy weight paper. (pg. 56)
Perfect binding	A method of binding loose-leaf pages where the pages and cover are glued together at the spine.
Perspective	A way of looking at or thinking about something. The way readers see and experience the events and feelings in the story. (pg. 42)
Picture books	A book containing many illustrations that is especially for children. (pg. 5)
Plagiarism	The practice of taking someone else's work or ideas and passing them off as one's own. (pg. 33)
Plot	The storyline of the text or the main events of the story written in sequence. (pg. 19)
Point of view (POV)	The opinions or feelings of a person involved in your story. (pg. 35)
Pre-assigned Control Number (PCN)	The number assigned to every book in the Library of Congress. (pg. 76)
Print run	The number of copies of a book, magazine, pamphlet, etc. that is printed at one time. (pg. 61)
Print-on-demand	A way of digitally printing books only as you need them, or after they are purchased. (pg. 58)
Promote	To actively support an author and further the progress and sales of a book. (pgs. 13, 92)
Proofreader	A person who finds and corrects mistakes in a story before the final copies are printed. (pgs. 33, 90)
Public domain	Creative material that is free for public use and is not protected by intellectual property laws such as copyright, trademark, or patent laws. (pg. 39)
Publication date	The date a book is published and made available to the public. (pg. 88)
Publicize	To make a person or something widely known. (pgs. 13, 92)
Purpose of a story	The most important thing a reader is supposed to walk away with like new information, a lesson, or a moral of the story. (pg. 27)
Rejection	The act of refusing to accept or buy something. (pg. 83)
Reporting	Giving a spoken or written account of something that one has observed, heard, done, or investigated. (pg. 32)
Retail price	The total price charged for a product sold to a customer, which includes what the item cost to make and the money made from the sale. (pg. 11)
RGB	RGB stands for "Red, Green, Blue." It refers to the three hues of light, that can mix together to form any color. (pgs. 64, 65)
Rhyming	When a word, syllable, or end of a line has the same sound as another. (pg. 37)
Royalty	A percentage of money paid to the author and illustrator for books sold. (pgs. 9, 15)
Saddle-stitch	A method of binding loose-leaf pages of a paperback book using staples down the middle or the gutter. (pg. 56)
Second person POV	The reader is invited to participate in the story and learns page-by-page what happens as a result of his or her actions. [Use of "You"] (pg. 36)
Self-publishing	Publishing a book independently and at your own expense. (pg. 7)
Setting	The place or type of surroundings where the story takes place. (pg. 20)
Spine (of book)	The outside edge where the pages are gathered and bound. (pg. 47)
Spread	A general description for a pair of facing pages, typically the left- and right-hand pages. (pg. 53)
Stereotype	An idea about how people will act based on the group to which they belong. (pg. 20)
Story map	A diagram that helps writers organize their thoughts by filling in the elements of a book or story, and identifying the story characters, plot, setting, problem, and solution. (pg. 24, 25, 26, 28, 29)
Storyboard	A sequence of sketches that show the significant changes of setting, dialog, action, and scenes in a book. (pg. 40)
Supporting characters	People or beings that are not the main focus of the story but contribute to the story in a significant way. (pg. 20)
Table of Contents	a list of the chapters or sections given at the front of a book or periodical. (pg. 52)
Text block	The pages or leaves of a book after they have been bound together. (pg. 47)
Text placement	Where the text is placed in the book. (pg. 73)
Text size	The height and width of text. (pg. 72)
Textless picture books	An illustrated picture book with no words—no written story. The illustration provides visual cues. (pg. 5)
Thesaurus	A book that lists words in groups of synonyms and related concepts. (pg. 34)

Theme	The main idea or topic of a story. (pg. 17)
Third person POV	The readers feel like someone is holding a camera and filming the events, or like they are listening to people gossip. [Use of "he," "she," "it," they"] (pg. 36)
Title	The title is a name or phrase that identifies or describes a book. (pg. 74)
Title page	The first interior page of the book, announcing the title, subtitle, author, illustrator, and publisher of the book. (pg. 75)
Traditional Publish House	A professional company that specializes in publishing books. (pg. 12)
Trim size	The final size of a printed page after excess edges have been cut off. (pg. 62)
Typeface	A family of fonts of a particular design. For example, the ARIAL font can be in typefaces such as regular, bold, italic, or condensed. (pg. 71)
Upload	The process of publishing content on the Internet. (pgs. 53, 54)
Watermark	A digital design placed on the cover or paper that makes it difficult to copy. (pg. 88)

51640182R00063

Made in the USA
Columbia, SC
22 February 2019